# DRAGON EMPIRES GAZETTEER

## A Pathfinder Campaign Setting Supplement

This book works best with the *Pathfinder Roleplaying Game Core Rulebook*.
Although suitable for play in any fantasy world, it is optimized for use in
the Pathfinder campaign setting.

## TABLE OF CONTENTS

## CREDITS

**Authors** • Matthew Goodall, Dave Gross, James Jacobs,
Steve Kenson, Michael Kortes, Colin McComb,
Rob McCreary, Richard Pett, F. Wesley Schneider,
Mike Shel, and Todd Stewart
**Cover Artist** • Wayne Reynolds
**Interior Artists** • Rayph Beisner, Dmitry Burmak,
Jon Hodgson, Jim Nelson, Eva Widermann,
and Ben Wooten

**Creative Director** • James Jacobs
**Senior Art Director** • Sarah E. Robinson
**Managing Editor** • F. Wesley Schneider
**Editing and Development** • Judy Bauer,
Christopher Carey, Patrick Renie, and James L. Sutter
**Editorial Assistance** • Jason Bulmahn, Rob McCreary,
Mark Moreland, Stephen Radney-MacFarland,
and Sean K Reynolds
**Graphic Designer** • Andrew Vallas
**Production Specialist** • Crystal Frasier

**Publisher** • Erik Mona
**Paizo CEO** • Lisa Stevens
**Vice President of Operations** • Jeffrey Alvarez
**Director of Sales** • Pierce Watters
**Sales Assistant** • Dylan Green
**Finance Manager** • Christopher Self
**Staff Accountant** • Kunji Sedo
**Technical Director** • Vic Wertz
**Campaign Coordinator** • Michael Brock

**Special Thanks** • The Paizo Customer Service,
Warehouse, and Website Teams

Paizo Publishing, LLC
7120 185th Ave NE, Ste 120
Redmond, WA 98052-0577
paizo.com

This product makes use of the *Pathfinder RPG Core Rulebook, Pathfinder RPG Advanced Player's Guide, Pathfinder RPG Bestiary, Pathfinder RPG Bestiary 2, Pathfinder RPG Bestiary 3, Pathfinder RPG Ultimate Combat,* and *Pathfinder RPG Ultimate Magic.* These rules can be found online as part of the Pathfinder Roleplaying Game Reference Document at paizo.com/pathfinderRPG/prd.

Printed in China.

# WELCOME TO THE DRAGON EMPIRES

Those who dwell in the Inner Sea region know the land as a vast swath of mountains and swamps, forests and plains, nations and wildlands, where one can expect to encounter a diverse range of challenges and mysteries. Be it the frontier lands of Varisia, the urban sprawl of Absalom, the frozen reaches of Irrisen, or the seemingly endless jungles and savannas of the Mwangi Expanse, the Inner Sea region presents an immense amount of opportunity for the curious and the brave.

Yet the Inner Sea is but one relatively small realm on Golarion. Other lands exist beyond the borders of Avistan and north Garund—the sunken continent of Azlant, the frozen terrors of the Crown of the World, the ancient nations that surround the Castrovin Sea,

and the mythical land of Vudra all draw adventurers from across the world. But when seekers of adventure and intrigue travel as far as one can go from the Inner Sea—whether having trekked across the polar ice to the north or endured the trials of an epic sea voyage—they arrive in a land of unfamiliar traditions and rich history. A land that stretches from the arctic circle to the north to well below the equator to the south. A land more than five times the area of the entire Inner Sea region, from the Linnorm Kingdoms to Sargava. These are the Dragon Empires.

## THE DRAGON EMPIRES

The continent of Tian Xia is a strange and exotic place to visitors from the west. Here, humans rub shoulders with fox and bird people, honor is an almost palpable force capable of deciding the fate of nations, and any stone or bush at the side of the road could potentially hide a fiercely protective guardian spirit. But one of the greatest differences between Tian Xia and the rest of the world is the way in which dragons interact with the people of the land.

In most parts of Golarion, including the Inner Sea region, dragons are recluses at best, and marauders at worst. The legends and tales of dragons devastating entire cities, gobbling up legions, and laying waste to nations are based all too closely on actual events. Even in the extremely rare cases when dragons seek to interact directly with humanoids without wreaking violence on a massive scale, the results are questionable—the ruler of the island nation of Hermea is a dragon, and his nation is composed of outwardly happy-seeming people, yet one does not have to look far under Hermea's surface to find evidence of trouble and discontent. And Hermea is the only such example at this time.

This is not to say that dragons never aid humans—just that, when such aid is given, it is almost always on a personal level. Dragons rarely, if ever, interact with the humanoid society of the Inner Sea region on a large scale other than to oppress or devastate.

This is not the case in Tian Xia. Here, the dragons that inhabit the land are not the reclusive metallics, murderous chromatics, or impartial primals. The dragons of these lands are known as imperial dragons, creatures inexorably tied to the balance of nature and civilization, ancestors and descendants, and heroes and villains. They do not avoid humanity—they

embrace it. Indeed, several of Tian Xia's most common gods may themselves be dragons. But even if these deities simply prefer the draconic form, the point remains the same. In Tian Xia, dragons serve as rulers, as advisors, and as gods. The five imperial families of Minkai were granted the divine right to rule by the goddess Shizuru in her draconic guise. The nation of Quain depends upon the magical aid granted by the powerful Celestial Dragon—aid greatly coveted by its neighbors Lingshen and Po Li. And in Xa Hoi, the people are ruled by a sovereign imperial dragon in human form. For these reasons and more, the lands of Tian Xia have long been known as the Dragon Empires.

## INSPIRATIONS

Golarion is a fantasy world, yet it is very much inspired by the real world. In the Inner Sea region, we drew upon real-world mythology and history to generate nations like Osirion, the Lands of the Linnorm Kings, Qadira, Varisia, and more. We did the same when developing the Dragon Empires.

In the following pages, you will find regions, deities, events, monsters, and people inspired by the myths and histories of numerous Asian analogs, such as Cambodia, China, Indonesia, Japan, Korea, Mongolia, Tibet, Vietnam, and more. Yet as you explore the Dragon Empires, it's worth keeping in mind one simple truth. Tian Xia is not Asia.

For many of the peoples, customs, deities, and regions, we've used real-world mythology and history as nothing more than a starting point. Just as Osirion isn't an exact duplicate of Egypt, neither is Minkai an exact replica of Japan. You'll find nations inspired by Korean legend that worship deities drawn from Chinese mythology, and entities from Japanese folklore living among societies modeled on Indonesian societies. While in the real world, you might not expect to see a ninja pop up in a Cambodian story, that's not the case in the Dragon Empires, where the traditions and myths of one region can significantly overlap with those of another. So when you explore the varied lands of Tian Xia, keep in mind that while we began with the real world during the creation of this book, where we ended up is Golarion. The concept of a Japan-inspired samurai taking up arms against an Indonesia-inspired undead monster really isn't all that outlandish when there are flying cities and nations ruled by krakens, after all!

Furthermore, countless movies helped to guide and inspire the development of the Dragon Empires—far too many to list here. Instead, presented here are a few mainstays—"required viewing," if you will, for anyone who's looking for more inspiration on running a Dragon Empires adventure.

### SPECIAL THANKS

The Dragon Empires have been a long time coming—we dropped the first hints of this realm early on, as soon as the very first installment of the very first Adventure Path, which featured a certain exiled family from the land of Minkai. And while we would continue to drop teasers and tidbits about this continent again and again, it took us nearly half a decade before the time was right to actually venture into the Dragon Empires. This book is something of a big deal for Paizo—in a lot of ways, it can be viewed as an entire new campaign setting. Yet we specifically chose to preserve a lot of links between the Dragon Empires and the Inner Sea region, because in truth, these lands are fundamentally part of Golarion. Just as an adventurer can do battle with a Tian sorcerer or adventure with a quirky tengu rogue in the Inner Sea, an adventurer in the Dragon Empires can run afoul of a Taldan assassin or visit a mysterious elven nation. This is on purpose—for the Dragon Empires are not so much their own setting as they are an immense expansion to Golarion as a whole.

And this is a good place to call out a few names and give out some special thanks to two guys who really helped get the ball rolling back in the dawn of Golarion—Mike McArtor and Nick Logue. While we were dropping hints of the Dragon Empires in "Burnt Offerings," they were already coming up with entire countries and nations for the far side of the world. They're the ones who gave the Dragon Empires their name—"Tian Xia." Both have moved on to other pursuits in life since those days, but we wanted to take the time to say thanks to them—this book's for the both of you!

*13 Assassins*, dir. Takashi Miike

**Big Trouble in Little China**, dir. John Carpenter

**Crouching Tiger, Hidden Dragon**, dir. Ang Lee

**Curse of the Golden Flower**, dir. Yimou Zhang

**Godzilla**, dir. Ishiro Honda

**The Hidden Fortress**, dir. Akira Kurosawa

**The Host**, dir. Joon-ho Bong

**House of Flying Daggers**, dir. Yimou Zhang

**The Legend of Drunken Master**, dir. Chia-Liang Liu and Jackie Chan

**Master of the Flying Guillotine**, dir. Yu Wang

**Once Upon a Time in China**, dir. Hark Tsui

**Ong-bak**, dir. Prachya Pinkaew

**Princess Mononoke**, dir. Hayao Miyazaki

**The Ring**, dir. Hideo Nakata

**Seven Samurai**, dir. Akira Kurosawa

**Spirited Away**, dir. Hayao Miyazaki

**The Warrior**, dir. Sung-su Kim

**Yojimbo**, dir. Akira Kurosawa

# Races of the Dragon Empires

What I found in Goka was beyond my expectations. I had thought to see the cold and formal Tian traders of Jalmeray. What I saw instead was chaos: ships and boats that beggared description, ornate carvings on everything, fruits and vegetables I had never before encountered. And the noise! Gone were the reserved faces of the Tians I was used to dealing with in the Inner Sea, replaced by a dizzying array of vibrant expressions and shouting voices. The market rivaled anything I'd seen in the West. My world—and my shipping schedule—had been turned upside down in a moment.

—Halvan Lorespun, trader of Absalom

The people of Tian Xia are nothing if not diverse. From the shapechanging kitsune to the avian tengus, or from the towering nagaji to the diminutive wayangs, those who dwell in the Dragon Empires cover a wide range of appearance, society, and belief. Even among humanity, by far the most widespread and populous of the Dragon Empires peoples, customs and appearances vary.

The most expansive and commonly encountered people of the Dragon Empires are humans, kitsune, nagaji, samsarans, tengus, and wayangs. While members of the non-human races listed can sometimes be found beyond Tian Xia's borders, they are most common on this continent. Likewise, foreign races like elves, dwarves, gnomes, halflings, half-elves, and half-orcs, while not common in the Dragon Empires, are not entirely unknown there.

## HUMANITY

While the people of the Inner Sea region often refer to Tians as members of a single ethnicity, they do so partially out of ignorance. In fact, there are seven distinct human ethnicities native to the Dragon Empires, all of whom share certain outlooks on life and philosophy—the concept of honor, the importance of ancestry, and great respect for dragons, for example. The people of Tian Xia symbolize these shared beliefs and convictions by appending the word "Tian" itself to their ethnicity, but in many more ways, these seven groups are themselves as diverse as any grouping of various races.

### TIAN-DANS

Tian-Dans are proud, often vocally so, of the fact that the blood of dragons runs in their veins. Whether or not this is true for the entirety of Xa Hoi's people is unclear, but certainly, the Dragon Kings of that nation can claim this, for they are themselves dragons. Tian-Dans find nothing strange in the concept of being ruled by dragons; as far as anyone can recall, this is as it has ever been. That the Dragon Kings themselves rarely appear outside of their human guise certainly helps, and indeed, many outlanders have spread rumors that the Dragon Kings are nothing more than humans. The Dragon Kings let these rumors go, for they have little interest in what outsiders think— the people of Xa Hoi know the truth of things.

Tian-Dans tend to be slender and lithe in build, with dark tan skin that approaches various shades of brown. Straight, black hair is by far the most common, although occasional natural streaks of color (blue, green, red, white, or yellow) are known and considered marks of importance. These hair highlights are often accompanied by similarly colored eyes (though silvery in place of white and golden in place of yellow) and a talent for sorcery. Tian-Dans are found most often in Xa Hoi.

**Languages:** Draconic, Tien

**Names:** Tian-Dans list their family names first, followed by their given names. *Example Family Names*: Cao, Chau, Dinh, Lam, Luong, Mai, Thuy, Trinh. *Example Female Given Names*: Bach Hien, Do Quyen, Hai Linh, Ngoc Yen, Que Xuan. *Example Male Given Names*: Huu Tai, Phung Trong, Thanh Liem, Toan Hao, Tuong Kinh.

### TIAN-DTANGS

"Respect the largest dragons and the smallest snakes," goes the Tian-Dtang proverb, "for the bite of either leaves you just as dead." Indeed, the people of Dtang Ma are full of helpful advice, but one cannot help but wonder whether they are offering time-honored wisdom, humor, or both. Tian-Dtangs take in the varied fortunes of life with a measure of serenity, good humor, and acceptance. Their villages, homes, and temples are as open as their lives, often being built with folding walls left open to the outside on good days. People come and go as they wish, and linger to visit in shaded courtyards or gardens, sipping sweet tea and exchanging tales and jokes.

Like Tian-Dans, Tian-Dtangs tend to have slender builds and tan skin. Black or dark brown hair is most common, although men often shave their scalps completely, or leave just a single lock of hair drawn into a topknot or woven into a long braid. Green or golden eyes sometimes replace the more common hues of brown or black. Tian-Dtangs are found most often in Dtang Ma.

**Languages:** Dtang, Tien

**Names:** Tian-Dtangs list their family names first, followed by their given names. *Example Family Names*: Dith, Meang, Muy, Nimol, Oum, Prum, Tep, Voeum. *Example Given Names*: Atith, Choum, Kosal, Maly, Prak, Rachany, Sarit, Vithu.

### TIAN-HWANS

Tian-Hwans were long oppressed by the people of Lung Wa, but now that Lung Wa has collapsed, the nation of Hwanggot is on the rise. Its people have always been ferociously proud and patriotic, and in the last century these personality traits have only increased. Tian-Hwans hold to traditional notions of distinct male and female roles, which may differ from those of other societies. For example, a greater proportion of Tian-Hwan warriors, generals, and scholars are female, with male roles among the Tian-Hwan tending toward professions like farming, craftsmanship, and artistic pursuits. Colors play a key role among the Tian-Hwans, and several have specific meanings. Red, for example, is generally thought of as an unlucky color because of its association with blood, while yellow is associated with protection against evil spirits and green symbolizes prosperity and peace.

As with their neighbors, the Tian-Dans and Tian-Dtangs, the Tian-Hwans tend to have thin builds and tan skin—of

the three, they also tend to be the shortest. Black or brown eyes are common but blue, violet, and even silvery eyes (considered particularly auspicious) are known. Their hair is generally black or dark brown. They are most commonly found in their ancestral homeland of Hwanggot.

**Languages**: Hwan, Tien

**Names**: Tian-Hwans list their family names first, followed by their given names. *Example Family Names*: Chae, Jun, Kam, Keun, Myo, Nang, Reong, Soh, Tak. *Example Female Given Names*: Chun-hei, Eun-kyung, Hei-ryung, Hyun-jae, Jae-hwa, Kyung-soon, Mi-sun, Soo-min, Yun-hi. *Example Male Given Names*: Cho-seol, Hyun-ki, Jung-hi, Kwan-song, Nam-kyu, Shin-il, Song-hwa, Yong-chul.

## TIAN-LAS

The people of the northern steppes of Hongal and the harsh plains and hills of Shaguang, Tian-Las are nomads, moving from place to place following the cycles of hunting and herding, and the seasonal thaws and floods from the mountains. They are known as expert riders and breeders of horses, but are also considered rough and uncivilized by the southern nations. Tian-Las are fierce and capable warriors, proud and quick to anger if offended.

Tian-Las have black and brown hair that tends to be coarse and curly. Their skin is typically relatively light. They often wear their hair in long braids; men wear these braids coiled beneath hats, while women cover theirs with veils or head-wraps, and warriors of both genders tuck their braids beneath peaked helms. Tian-Las have a higher percentage of meat in their diet, much of it horseflesh, and likewise consume mare's milk both in tea and fermented into a drink called *aareg*.

**Languages**: Hon-la, Tien

**Names**: Tian-Las generally have only a given name, although in some cases that given name can consist of two words—they do not traditionally keep family names. *Example Female Given Names*: Alerdene, Bayandash, Narantuyaa, Odval, Surenchinua. *Example Male Given Names*: Batsaikhan, Enqbatu, Gansukh, Qorchi, Tomorbaatar.

## TIAN-MINS

The people of Minkai display the widest range in eye color among the people of the Dragon Empires, from the typical black or brown to blue, green, violet, amber, orange, red-orange, and even gold. Some believe a person's eye color determines or reflects her personality and aptitudes, and therefore her place in life. Pale skin is considered the most attractive, so many Tian-Mins (particularly women) wear white face-powder and paint their eyelids and lips a darker shade to enhance contrast. Tattoos are popular among Tian-Mins, and among certain organizations such body art is used to denote station and power as much as for decor. Images of mystical creatures like dragons, kami, kirin, oni, and undead spirits are typical subjects, although colorful animals and plants are common as well. Straight black hair is the most common. Women grow their hair long, and often wear it coiled or pinned beneath a headdress or veil; male hairstyles are typically shorter, with longer hair indicating higher status. Warriors and nobles of both genders wear their hair in a topknot. Tian-Mins tend to be as fastidious about personal cleanliness and appearance as their wealth and station allow, bathing daily, wearing perfume, and adorning themselves in the finest clothes they can. Honor is of great import to Tian-Mins, as is respect for elders and superiors in both family and government.

**Languages**: Minkaian, Tien

**Names**: Tian-Mins list their family names first, followed by their given names. *Example Family Names*: Entobe, Kaneka, Nakayama, Noro, Sentagawa, Ueshima. *Example Female Given Names*: Ayuna, Hiriko, Kaede, Kasuri, Meguma, Reiko, Umie. *Example Male Given Names*: Hayato, Hisashi, Hitoshi, Ishirou, Kousei, Shirota, Yoshiro, Yuto, Zaiho.

## TIAN-SHUS

Tian-Shus are the most populous and most commonly encountered ethnicity in Tian Xia. They have dusky skin, almond-shaped eyes (predominantly brown and black in hue), and straight black or dark brown hair. Tian-Shus tend toward slight, slender builds, in contrast to the northern Tian-Las. Lower class Tian-Shus dress in simple cotton or linen trousers and tunics, while those able to afford them prefer fine silk robes, brightly colored and elaborately embroidered with images of dragons and other mystical creatures. Tian-Shus are an orderly, class-conscious people. Society is based around a natural order mandated by the gods, and everyone has a place and role in this intricate structure. Dragons rule at the top of this system, and are in some ways viewed as equals to the gods themselves. There is room for advancement—Tian-Shus believe strongly in the recognition of individual merit and achievement—but there are also certain roles decreed by fate, which must be accepted. When everyone is in the proper place, society is harmonious and productive. When the natural order is disrupted, chaos ensues until it can be righted once again.

**Languages**: Tien

**Names**: Tian-Shus list their family names first, followed by their given names. *Example Family Names*: Bai, Chun, Fong, Gua, Jiang, Mai, Shan, Tsui. *Example Female Given Names*: Chao, Fei, Meilin, Qiao, Rui, Zhi. *Example Male Given Names*: Bi, Dawei, Jianguo, Shuo, Xun, Zhen.

## TIAN-SINGS

Found primarily in the so-called Wandering Isles of Minata, Tian-Sings have the darkest of Tian skin tones, ranging from tan to dark brown. Their dark hair has a greater degree

of natural wave, although it is usually worn short (or even shaved completely) to combat the heat of Minata's endless summers. Tian-Sings have round faces similar to those of Tian-Hwans, but with sharper noses and cheekbones. They emphasize these traits with jewelry, and are quite fond of piercings through the ears, nose, and lips—facial tattoos are common as well. Unlike the colorful body art of the Tian-Mins, Tian-Sing tattoos tend to be geometric or pictographic and single-colored. Clothing, on the other hand, is brightly colored, with similar geometric patterns and prints, but in many Tian-Sing societies clothing is considered all but optional, again, as a result of Minata's hot climate.

**Languages:** Minatan, Tien

**Names:** The typical Tian-Sing has only a single given name and no family name. *Example Female Given Names:* Indah, Lestari, Nirmala, Sangati, Udara. *Example Male Given Names:* Budi, Hamengku, Kusuma, Purnoma, Suryo.

# FOREIGNERS

The Tien term *xijan* means "westerner" or "western people," but also means "foreigner" or even "barbarian" depending on inflection or context. The people of Tian Xia are aware of the existence of Avistan and other distant lands, but the vast expanse of the Okaiyo Ocean, the perils of crossing the Crown of the World, and the shield of the Wall of Heaven work quite well to keep the Dragon Empires relatively isolated from the rest of Golarion.

## HUMANS

Humans from across Golarion often find their way to Tian Xia—Keleshite merchants from Katapesh and Qadira, Garundi wanderers and explorers eager to find new sea trade routes, and even bands of Kellid and Ulfen barbarians from the Crown of the World. Varisian caravans often make the northern crossing as well, and Vudrani monks and martial artists come to the Dragon Empires seeking legendary teachers. Mwangi are rarely seen, but are both feared and respected because of their similarity to the "sky spirits" of Shaguang. Tians sometimes refer to Chelaxians as *xiaoguai*, "little devils," and look upon them with even more suspicion than most. Taldans are widely known in Tian Xia, thanks to the growing influence of Amanandar and the increased presence of Taldan merchants and aristocrats in Goka.

## DWARVES

The few dwarves from Avistan and elsewhere who find their way to Tian Xia usually do so on an individual basis, traveling with larger groups of adventurers, merchants, or explorers. Very few larger groups of dwarves travel to Tian Xia, although stories of extended families making the underground journey through the Darklands persist.

## ELVES

While elves have lived in the forested realm of Jinin for thousands of years, they have traditionally remained under a self-imposed isolation. Nevertheless, elves are perhaps the most well known of the western races, after humans, in the Dragon Empires. Since the fall of Lung Wa and Jinin's rise to power once again as an independent nation, elves are growing more common in certain nearby regions like Amanandar and Shokuro. The elven lifestyle and love of beauty meshes well with Tian-Min aesthetics. Elves also tend to understand and enjoy the company of samsarans, for both have a similar outlook on life.

## GNOMES

It is no wonder that gnomes, ever driven to experience new things, often find their way into Tian Xia, exploring the lands and peoples there. Yet, like dwarves, gnomes generally arrive individually, and rarely settle in one place for long. Gnomes are a curiosity in the lands of the east, and are often confused with kami or similar creatures. Although they are of a similar stature to wayangs, these two races do not get along well—when gnomes and wayangs meet, insults and even violence are common results.

## HALF-ELVES

Although the elves of Jinin remain largely clannish and separate from the rest of the Dragon Empires, elven blood has slowly filtered into the populace of what was once central Lung Wa. In the old days of that empire, many half-elves found their way into Imperial service, eager to improve their lots in life and to put their natural talents to good use. This led to the common image of half-elves as smooth-talking bureaucrats, a stereotype that remains in Lingshan, Shokuro, and Quain. In Zi Ha, some half-elves pursue a different path, seeking spiritual enlightenment and peace at one of the many samsaran monasteries or temples.

## HALF-ORCS

The few half-orcs found in Tian Xia typically arrive in Ordu-Aganhei after making the journey across the Crown of the World, where they find opportunities among the Tien-La nomads, who value their endurance and ferocity. While the general Tian obsession with beauty typically limits half-orcs' opportunities throughout much of the Dragon Empires, those who have abandoned or avoided their ancestral ferocity often find kindred spirits among the equally unusual-looking nagaji, and as such the half-orc populace among cities and villages in Nagajor is on the rise.

## HALFLINGS

Wanderlust and close ties with western human communities have led some of halflings to the shores of Tian Xia, as either servants or explorers in their own right.

## RANDOM STARTING AGES

| Race | Adulthood | Intuitive[1] | Self-Taught[2] | Trained[3] |
|---|---|---|---|---|
| Kitsune | 15 years | +1d4 | +1d6 | +2d6 |
| Nagaji | 20 years | +1d6 | +2d6 | +3d6 |
| Samsaran | 60 years | +4d6 | +6d6 | +8d6 |
| Tengu | 15 years | +1d4 | +1d6 | +2d6 |
| Wayang | 40 years | +4d6 | +5d6 | +6d6 |

1   This category includes barbarians, oracles, rogues, and sorcerers.

2   This category includes bards, cavaliers, fighters, gunslingers, paladins, rangers, summoners, and witches.

3   This category includes alchemists, clerics, druids, inquisitors, magi, monks, and wizards.

## AGING EFFECTS

| Race | Middle Age | Old | Venerable | Maximum Age |
|---|---|---|---|---|
| Kitsune | 32 years | 50 years | 65 years | 65 + 3d12 years |
| Nagaji | 60 years | 90 years | 120 years | 120 + 3d20 years |
| Samsaran | 150 years | 200 years | 250 years | 250 + 6d% years |
| Tengu | 35 years | 53 years | 70 years | 70 + 2d20 years |
| Wayang | 100 years | 150 years | 200 years | 200 + 1d% years |

## RANDOM HEIGHT AND WEIGHT

| Race | Base Height | Base Weight | Modifier | Weight Multiplier |
|---|---|---|---|---|
| Kitsune, male | 4 ft. 10 in. | 100 lbs. | 2d8 | × 5 lbs. |
| Kitsune, female | 4 ft. 5 in. | 85 lbs. | 2d8 | × 5 lbs. |
| Nagaji, male | 5 ft. 9 in. | 180 lbs. | 2d10 | × 7 lbs. |
| Nagaji, female | 5 ft. 6 in. | 160 lbs. | 2d10 | × 7 lbs. |
| Samsaran, male | 5 ft. 4 in. | 110 lbs. | 2d8 | × 5 lbs. |
| Samsaran, female | 5 ft. 6 in. | 110 lbs. | 2d8 | × 5 lbs. |
| Tengu, male | 4 ft. 0 in. | 65 lbs. | 2d6 | × 3 lbs. |
| Tengu, female | 3 ft. 10 in. | 55 lbs. | 2d6 | × 3 lbs. |
| Wayang, male | 3 ft. 0 in. | 35 lbs. | 2d4 | × 1 lbs. |
| Wayang, female | 2 ft. 10 in. | 30 lbs. | 2d4 | × 1 lbs. |

Some have chosen to leave behind their former ties, and spend their lives visiting the eastern lands or settle in its more cosmopolitan places. Even here, halflings tend to live in the shadows cast by humans—so the few found in Tian Xia are in cities like Ordu-Aganhei and Goka.

## AASIMARS

Tianjing, the Beloved of the Heavens, is often seen by the Tians as being synonymous with the *tianjans*—the "heaven people," also known as aasimars. Like western aasimars, tianjans have a sacred celestial heritage. Aasimar children are often raised in temples and trained as priests, monks, or sacred warriors. They are expected to humbly accept and take up their destined roles, although some rebel against these expectations, seeking their own paths.

## HOBGOBLINS

While goblins and bugbears are relatively rare in Tian Xia, the same cannot be said of hobgoblins. The broken lands east of the Shaguang Desert have long been infested by hobgoblins, and with the fall of Lung Wa and the rise of several charismatic and powerful hobgoblin warlords, the nation of Kaoling has been growing in size and influence over the past century. Today one of the most notorious of the Successor States, Kaoling is home to unknown tens of thousands of hobgoblins who threaten all lands they border, from the windswept southern regions of Hongal to the northern plains of Lingshan. Like their western cousins, hobgoblins in Tian Xia are cruel, militaristic, and cunning.

## NEW RACES

The five new PC race options presented on the following pages have additional rules, particularly for advancement options, in both this book's companion volume, *Pathfinder Player Companion: Dragon Empires Primer*, and the upcoming *Advanced Race Guide*. Random starting ages, aging effects, and heights and weights for these races are summarized on the charts above. See pages 168–169 in the *Pathfinder RPG Core Rulebook* for notes on how to read and use these tables.

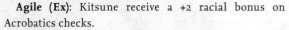

# KITSUNE

The kitsune are a race of shapechanging fox folk, known throughout the Dragon Empires for their love of art, beauty, and whimsical trickery.

**Physical Description**: A kitsune has two forms—a single human form and its true form, that of a humanoid fox. In their human forms, kitsune tend toward quickness and lithe beauty. In all forms they possess golden, amber, or brilliant blue eyes. In their true forms, they are covered with a downy coat of auburn fur, although more exotic coloration is possible.

**Society**: Kitsune society is enigmatic, as kitsune prize loyalty among their friends but delight in good-natured mischief and trickery. Kitsune take pleasure in the pursuit of creative arts and in all forms of competition, especially the telling of stories interwoven with tall tales and falsehoods.

**Relations**: Kitsune deal well with elves and samsarans, but their reputation as tricksters follows them when they interact with other races. Many kitsune, particularly those who dwell in mixed-race societies, choose to hide their true natures and pose as humans in public.

**Alignment and Religion**: Kitsune tend to be neutral, or of alignments with a neutral component. Most kitsune worship Daikitsu, the goddess of craftsmanship, but they also often worship Shelyn and Lao Shu Po.

**Adventurers**: Keenly interested in adding their own names to the myths and legends of explorers and heroes of old, Kitsune adventurers range across Tian Xia.

**Female Names**: Ayaki, Jiyoki, Kyomi, Miyaro, Shinyai, Yulai

**Male Names**: Chankotu, Imhakaru, Kyrsaku, Namkitu, Yanyeeku

## KITSUNE RACIAL TRAITS

All kitsune are humanoids with the kitsune and shapechanger subtypes. They have the following racial traits.

**+2 Dexterity, +2 Charisma, −2 Strength**: Kitsune are agile and companionable, but tend to be physically weak.

**Medium**: Kitsune are Medium creatures and have no bonuses or penalties due to their size.

**Normal Speed**: Kitsune have a base speed of 30 feet.

**Low-Light Vision (Ex)**: Kitsune can see twice as far as humans in conditions of dim light.

**Change Shape (Su)**: A kitsune can assume the appearance of a single human form of the same sex—this form is static, and cannot be changed each time the kitsune assumes this form. A kitsune in human form cannot make its bite attack, but gains a +10 racial bonus on Disguise checks made to appear human. Changing from human to kitsune shape is a standard action. This ability otherwise functions as *alter self*, save that the kitsune does not adjust its ability scores.

**Agile (Ex)**: Kitsune receive a +2 racial bonus on Acrobatics checks.

**Kitsune Feats**: At higher levels, kitsune can select special feats to grant them additional powers, such as the ability to change shape into an actual fox. These feats are presented in this book's companion volume, the *Dragon Empires Primer*.

**Kitsune Magic (Ex/Sp)**: Kitsune add +1 to the DC of any saving throws against enchantment spells that they cast. Kitsune with a Charisma score of 11 or higher gain the following spell-like ability: 3/day—*dancing lights*.

**Natural Weapon (Ex)**: A kitsune has a bite attack in its natural form. This bite does a base of 1d4 points of damage on a hit. This is a primary attack, or a secondary attack if the kitsune wields a manufactured weapon.

**Languages**: Kitsune begin play speaking Tien and Senzar. Kitsune with high Intelligence scores can choose bonus languages from the following: any human tongue, Aklo, Celestial, Elven, Gnome, Nagaji, Samsaran, Sylvan, Tengu, and Wayang.

## NAGAJI

Bred in the ancient past by nagas seeking a servitor race that combined the loyalty of a slave with the versatility of the human form, the nagaji have long since developed into a vibrant and proud race.

**Physical Description:** The reptilian nagaji have scaly flesh—these scales are typically green, gray, or brown in hue, with colorful ridges of red, blue, or orange on their skulls or backs. Their ears and noses are flat, almost to the point of being nonexistent, while their eyes are those of serpents, ranging widely in color but tending toward golds, reds, yellows, and other warm hues.

**Society:** Nagaji society places honor, devotion, and dedication above all else. Less charitable observers from outside such societies might call the nagaji "born slaves," but the nagaji do not think of themselves as slaves to their naga overlords, and point to the fact that they are free to make their own life decisions, even to leave Nagajor if they wish. Furthermore, when a naga oversteps its bounds as ruler of its people, the nagaji are no strangers to resistance or outright rebellion, as even an idle study of Nagajor's history reveals.

**Relations:** For their part, nagaji regard humans as violent expansionists not to be trusted as political neighbors or allies. They tend to see kitsune and tengus as too capricious and mischievous to trust, but they grudgingly respect the samsarans' wisdom. Wayangs are mistrusted as well, for their apparent lack of a strong national heritage worries and confounds the nagaji.

**Alignment and Religion:** Most nagaji are lawful neutral, but nagaji of any alignment are possible. While many non-nagaji believe they worship their naga lords as gods, this is not true—yet religion does play a secondary role in nagaji society to civic obedience. The fact that the patron deity of the nagaji, Nalinivati, goddess of sorcery, is said to have been the first ruler of Nagajor speaks much to this philosophy.

**Adventurers:** Nagaji are often drawn to lives of adventure out of a desire to prove themselves to their naga masters, or to prove their own worth outside of this racial obligation. Strong of body and personality, nagaji excel as sorcerers, fighters, and for the right personality, serve exceptionally well as paladins.

**Female Names:** Hskori, Korovati, Reomava, Resavati, Sellaweti, Yesmava, Zehameti

**Male Names:** Hskoro, Iltame, Nagagorjo, Rasamoro, Seme, Sulmavate, Yesmoro

### NAGAJI RACIAL TRAITS

All nagaji are humanoids with the reptilian subtype. They have the following racial traits.

**+2 Strength, +2 Charisma, −2 Intelligence:** Nagaji are strong and have forceful personalities, but tend to ignore logic and mock scholastic pursuits.

**Medium:** Nagaji are Medium creatures and have no bonuses or penalties due to their size.

**Normal Speed:** Nagaji have a base speed of 30 feet.

**Low-Light Vision (Ex):** Nagaji can see twice as far as humans in conditions of dim light.

**Armored Scales (Ex):** Nagaji have a +1 natural armor bonus from their scaly flesh.

**Resistant (Ex):** Nagaji receive a +2 racial saving throw bonus against mind-affecting effects and poison.

**Serpent's Sense (Ex):** Nagaji receive a +2 racial bonus on Handle Animal checks against reptiles, and a +2 racial bonus on Perception checks.

**Languages:** Nagaji begin play speaking Nagaji and Tien. Nagaji with high Intelligence scores can choose bonus languages from the following: any human tongue, Abyssal, Aklo, Celestial, Draconic, Giant, Infernal, Samsaran, Senzar, Sylvan, Tengu, and Wayang.

## SAMSARANS

Capable of recalling the lessons and failings of their previous incarnations, the samsarans seek to live lives of balance and enlightenment in order to ensure they are reborn upon death to continue their trek through history.

**Physical Description:** Samsarans appear as humans with pale blue skin, solid white eyes with no pupil or iris, and dark hair. A samsaran's blood is crystal clear, like the water of a pure mountain spring.

**Society:** Samsarans prefer to live simple lives of reflection, scholarship, and worship. They try to live their lives free of the ambitions and greed that mortality often imposes, since they view their lives as only the latest incarnation of many to come. Any accomplishments left undone in this current life can surely be achieved in the next, or the one after that. Samsarans' memories of their past lives are not complete—they most often feel like half-remembered dreams. Samsarans can give birth, yet they do not give birth to samsarans—instead, they birth human children. Typically, samsarans give up their children not long after birth to be raised in human society, where the children grow and live their lives normally. Upon death, such offspring sometimes reincarnate as samsaran children, if they lived their lives in keeping with harmony. While most samsarans who die also reincarnate as samsaran children, this is not always the case. When a samsaran has utterly failed at maintaining harmony in her current life, or when she has succeeded perfectly at it, her soul instead travels to the Great Beyond to receive its final, long-delayed reward or doom. Samsarans do not keep family names, but often retain the names of their previous one or two incarnations, regardless of gender, as a sort of replacement for a family name to honor their previous lives' accomplishments or to remind them of their past shames.

**Relations:** Humans and others often misunderstand samsarans' nature. Many fear or even hate samsarans' unusual association with death, thinking them to be strangely cursed souls at best or vengeful spirits made flesh at worst.

**Alignment and Religion:** Most samsarans are lawful good—but samsarans of any alignment are possible. Deeply religious, the majority of samsarans take patron deities even if they aren't clerics, with Tsukiyo, the patron of the samsaran race, being the most commonly worshiped.

**Adventurers:** Adventuring allows samsarans to see the world's wonders, deepens their understanding of life, and lets them visit places half remembered from their previous lives.

**Female Names:** Chimi, Mindu, Nalita, Rema, Sonitri, Treeni, Yeshing

**Male Names:** Agyen, Bakji, Dakash, Henar, Puran, Sonan, Thukten

## SAMSARAN RACIAL TRAITS

All samsarans are humanoids with the samsaran subtype. They have the following racial traits.

**+2 Intelligence, +2 Wisdom, –2 Constitution:** Samsarans are insightful and strong-minded, but their bodies are frail.

**Medium:** Samsarans are Medium creatures and have no bonuses or penalties due to their size.

**Normal Speed:** Samsarans have a base speed of 30 feet.

**Low-Light Vision (Ex):** Samsarans can see twice as far as humans in conditions of dim light.

**Lifebound (Ex):** Samsarans gain a +2 racial bonus on all saving throws made to resist death effects, saving throws against negative energy effects, Fortitude saves made to remove negative levels, and Constitution checks made to stabilize if reduced to negative hit points.

**Samsaran Magic (Sp):** Samsarans with a Charisma score of 11 or higher gain the following spell-like abilities: 1/day—*comprehend languages*, *deathwatch*, and *stabilize*. The caster level for these effects is equal to the samsaran's level.

**Shards of the Past (Ex):** A samsaran's past lives grant her bonuses on two particular Knowledge skills. A samsaran chooses two Knowledge skills—she gains a +2 racial bonus on both of these skills, and they are treated as class skills regardless of what class she actually takes.

**Languages:** Samsarans begin play speaking Samsaran and Tien. Samsarans with high Intelligence scores can choose bonus languages from the following: any human tongue, Abyssal, Aquan, Auran, Celestial, Draconic, Giant, Ignan, Infernal, Nagaji, Senzar, Tengu, Terran, and Wayang.

# TENGUS

Long oppressed as a poor underclass within human nations and viewed as thieves and dishonorable scoundrels, many raven-headed tengus yearn to break free of these caste-restrictions and stereotypes.

**Physical Description**: Tengus are roughly humanoid in shape, save that they possess heads akin to those of ravens or crows. Like those birds, they have a coat of deep black feathers, though color variations of brown and blue-black exist. They have the scaled, clawed feet of their avian forebears and scaly but humanoid hands to match, though they lack wings and only their beaks possess the capacity for use as a natural weapon. Tengus often dress in loose, simple clothing bound tighter around their arms and ankles, with only a small bit of adornment. Among their own kind they relax these styles and flaunt whatever adornments they can find, purchase, or pilfer, especially favoring rings on both fingers and toes.

**Society**: Long oppressed and relegated to the margins of larger, multi-species societies, tengus remain an insular and secretive people. Though rarely sharing their culture and its workings with outsiders, they happily integrate aspects from other cultures in the same way crows pilfer bits of twine and shiny baubles. Tengus revere their elders, and when they gather together, they defer leadership to age just as much as to experience. The tengu homeland is the nation of Kwanlai, a land still struggling with its independence after the fall of imperial Lung Wa.

**Relations**: Long after the fall of imperial Lung Wa, many other races still view tengus as petty thieves, compulsive liars, and sinister conspirators, even though that perception is largely a survival of Lung Wa's history of oppression and social abuse of its tengu citizens.

**Alignment and Religion**: Tengus usually have a neutral component to their alignment, with a fairly even spread between law and chaos or good and evil. Hei Feng, the Duke of Thunder, is the patron deity of the tengu race.

**Adventurers**: Tengus typically become adventurers who seek wealth and glory beyond the poverty of their roots. However, while many assume such lifestyles to escape the stereotypes of their race, just as many do so to revel in the role of the "shifty, sneaky tengu rogue."

**Female Names**: Aikio, Cheetchu, Kankai, Mikacha, Zhanyae
**Male Names**: Chuko, Pezzack, Taicho, Tchoyoitu, Xaikon

## TENGU RACIAL TRAITS

All tengus are humanoids with the tengu subtype. They have the following racial traits.

**+2 Dexterity, +2 Wisdom, –2 Constitution**: Tengus are fast and observant, but relatively fragile and delicate.

**Medium**: Tengus are Medium creatures and have no bonuses or penalties due to their size.

**Normal Speed**: Tengus have a base speed of 30 feet.

**Low-Light Vision (Ex)**: Tengus can see twice as far as humans in conditions of dim light.

**Sneaky (Ex)**: Tengus gain a +2 racial bonus on Perception and Stealth.

**Gifted Linguist (Ex)**: Tengus gain a +4 racial bonus on Linguistics checks, and learn two languages each time they gain a rank in Linguistics instead of just a single language.

**Swordtrained (Ex)**: Tengus are trained from birth in swordplay, and as a result are automatically proficient with swordlike weapons.

**Natural Weapon (Ex)**: Tengus possess a bite attack that deals 1d3 points of damage on a hit. This is a primary attack, or a secondary attack if the tengu wields a manufactured weapon.

**Languages**: Tengus begin play speaking Tengu and Tien. Tengus with high Intelligence scores can choose any language as a bonus language.

# WAYANGS

Wayangs are trespassers upon Golarion, a fact the world seems ferociously committed to reminding them. Tied to the eternal night of the Plane of Shadow, wayangs slipped between the boundaries between worlds during the Age of Darkness, finding shadow-engulfed Golarion well suited to their tastes. As the centuries-long night passed, however, wayangs found themselves trapped upon a world turning inhospitable under the light of a newly emerged sun.

**Physical Description:** Wayangs are short and lean, similar in stature to gnomes, though tending toward darker, more muted colorations. Their features are sharp, and their skin tones range from shades of twilight plum and dark gray to depthless black. Most undergo ritual scarification and tattooing from a young age.

**Society:** Forming small, tightly knit tribes, wayangs live a communal existence, sharing what they have with their friends and families. Their culture seems morbid to most outsiders, one that idealizes a shadowy state of nonbeing while demonizing the fierce clarity of light.

**Relations:** Most wayang tribes do their best to avoid the notice of Golarion's populace. To them, the hunting jaguar, the sharp-taloned hawk, and the greedy human are relentless co-conspirators, seeking to exploit, torment, and kill the wayangs. Only through their nimbleness and secretiveness have wayangs survived.

**Alignment and Religion:** Wayang culture guides its members toward neutrality; wayangs avoid the conflicts of others and seek the balance found in shadow, although they can be of any alignment. Lao Shu Po is the patron of the wayangs, although many wayangs think of her as a curse upon their people rather than a blessing.

**Adventurers:** Sometimes the folktales and warnings of wayang elders have the opposite of their intended effect, fascinating bold youths with stories of the countless creatures and brilliant worlds beyond their hidden communities.

**Female Names:** Clouei, Duskade, Ebnalli, Eclis, Shadni, Twilaka, Wahmisti

**Male Names:** Ballipho, Daratas, Glomintar, Oboskursuma, Shawarto, Umbrutari, Veilwar

## WAYANG RACIAL TRAITS

All wayangs are humanoids with the wayang subtype. They have the following racial traits.

**+2 Dexterity, +2 Intelligence, –2 Wisdom:** Wayangs are nimble and cagey, but their perception of the world is clouded by shadows.

**Small:** Wayangs are Small creatures and gain a +1 size bonus to their AC, a +1 size bonus on attack rolls, a –1 penalty on their combat maneuver checks and to CMD, and a +4 size bonus on Stealth checks.

**Slow Speed:** Wayangs have a base speed of 20 feet.

**Darkvision:** Wayangs can see in the dark up to 60 feet.

**Light and Dark (Su):** Once per day as an immediate action, a wayang can treat positive and negative energy effects as if the wayang were an undead creature, taking damage from positive energy and healing damage from negative energy. This ability lasts for 1 minute once activated.

**Lurker (Ex):** Wayangs gain a +2 racial bonus on Perception and Stealth checks.

**Shadow Magic (Ex/Sp):** Wayangs add +1 to the DC of any saving throws against spells of the shadow subschool that they cast. Wayangs with a Charisma score of 11 or higher also gain the following spell-like abilities: 1/day—*ghost sound*, *pass without trace*, and *ventriloquism*. The caster level for these effects is equal to the wayang's level. The DC for these spells is equal to 10 + the spell's level + the wayang's Charisma modifier.

**Shadow Resistance (Ex):** Wayangs get a +2 racial saving throw bonus against spells of the shadow subschool.

**Languages:** Wayangs begin play speaking Tien and Wayang. Wayangs with high Intelligence scores can choose from the following: any human tongue, Abyssal, Aklo, Draconic, Goblin, Infernal, Nagaji, Samsaran, Senzar, and Tengu.

# Regions of the Dragon Empires

From the high mountains of the Wall of Heaven to the trackless jungles of Valashmai, our land is fair and forbidding, its proud history buried in time. If you seek adventure in a trackless desert, it is yours. Should you wish to scale peaks that touch the homes of the gods, you need only seek them out. Do you wish to plunder an ancient dragon's tomb, or brave the horrors on the western shores of the Sea of Ghosts, or seek insight into your past life hidden among the spires of Zi Ha? Find your courage and go. Trade, magic, knowledge, history: this is a land of opportunity for those who have the desire to seize it.

—Rasit Nakry, noble of Dtang Ma

Although the Dragon Empires have been populated by humans for thousands of years, the land was not always under the rule of the Tians. When Azlant was at its height on the opposite side of the world, Tian Xia was populated only by spirits and dragons. Earthfall devastated the western hemisphere of Golarion, but did not directly damage Tian Xia. Nonetheless, the land shook with tremors and suffered numerous tsunamis along its coastlines from the ancient catastrophe. And in Valashmai, great antipodal volcanoes rose from the jungle—these volcanoes remain today as a subtle but lasting scar of the thunder that struck the other side of the world.

Historical and religious records are frustratingly vague at pinpointing when the first humans arrived in Tian Xia. Some documents indicate that the earliest of these were refugees from Azlant, or expansionistic explorers from Ninshabur, but others suggest that the first humans rose spontaneously, either as the result of a powerful race dabbling with the creation of life or the intervention of the gods. The most commonly accepted explanation, though, is an ancient mass incarnation of humanity—scholars have linked this hypothetical event to the destruction of Azlant, theorizing that a vast number of the Azlanti slain during Earthfall were reincarnated on the opposite side of the world, but without any of their memories of ancient Azlant. These humans would have been fresh souls, blank slates with no burden of sin, and more importantly, beyond the notice of the aboleths who struck out so potently against Azlant's hubris. Whatever the source of this sudden influx of humanity, it would be many centuries before a human empire rose in Tian Xia— the empire of Yixing, establishing what most people in Tian Xia regard as the Age of Ascendancy.

## CALENDAR

As in the Inner Sea region, many different calendars exist in the Dragon Empires. Some are used only on a small scale by single nations, such as the Mithral Count in Jinin, while others are ancient and have fallen away from common use. More common calendars include the Sovereign Scroll, used exclusively by the Dragon Emperors of Xa Hoi to track time back to the genesis of their nation, or even the Inner Sea's own Absalom Reckoning, which is seeing increased use in Goka and Hongal because of growing western influences there.

The most commonly accepted calendar in the Dragon Empires, and the one in the widest use by its people, is the Imperial Calendar, established over 7,000 years ago by the empire of Yixing. This calendar is based on the year this first empire was founded, and corresponds to year –2500 in Absalom Reckoning). To convert a date from the Imperial Calendar to Absalom Reckoning, simply subtract 2,500 from the year—thus, the current date in the Imperial Calendar, 7211 IC, corresponds to the year 4711 AR.

## DRAGON EMPIRES TIMELINE

The Imperial Calendar organizes history into three different ages. The time before the Age of Ashes predates humanity's presence on the continent—it is known as the "Age of Dragons," for common belief is that the continent was ruled in those ancient days by imperial dragons who had been tasked by the gods themselves to care for the world until humanity could claim it as their birthright. All dates in this timeline follow the Imperial Calendar.

### AGE OF ASHES

| Date | Event |
|---|---|
| –2793 | Earthfall. While Tian Xia is not directly impacted by this catastrophic fall of stars from the sky, powerful tsunamis reshape the continent's coastline, and the Chenlun Mountains, located at the antipode of the greatest strikes against Azlant, rise up in a storm of volcanoes. Ashes blot out the sun for years, ushering in an impossibly long winter. The onslaught from land, sea, and air devastates the land, especially the southern reptilian empire of Valashai. The ashes of Azlant hang physically in the skies for years—but metaphorically, they loom for a thousand more. |
| –2343 | Elves fleeing from Celwynvian and the devastation of Earthfall finally complete their several-hundred-year journey through the Darklands. Following the "roots" of a vast lode of mithral up from Sekamina, the elves emerge in central Tian Xia and found the nation of Jinin. |
| –1794 | Humanity finally begins to rebuild throughout Golarion. In Tian Xia, humanity rises with shocking speed, although it will be nearly 2,000 years before the first human empire is founded. |
| –1203 | The first contact between humanity and the nagaji results in a nameless war that taints relations between both races for over 2,000 years. |
| –1102 | In distant Garund, Old-Mage Jatembe and his Ten Magic Warriors bring the light of learning back to the world. His discoveries would eventually lead to the founding of the empire of Shory. |
| –384 | The first khan rises to power in Hongal, a towering man named Budugan who claimed to be half giant. |
| –379 | When Budugan is slain by treacherous kin, the first Tian-La tribe fractures into dozens of smaller tribes— it will be many centuries before a large tribe once again rises on the tundras and steppes of Hongal. |
| –24 | Mount Shibotai erupts, blanketing much of Tian Xia in ash and evoking the ancient fears of Earthfall at the dawn of the Age of Ashes. When the ashes spewed by this smaller (yet still devastating) disaster clear after a mere few months, humanity realizes that the Age of Ashes is coming to a close—the resulting surge in hope is a major factor in the rise of Yixing's power. |

## Age of Ascendancy

| Date | Event |
| --- | --- |
| 1 | The empire of Yixing is established, ushering in a new age of prosperity and exploration across Tian Xia. |
| 98 | The celestial keepers of Tianjing cede rule of that land to their aasimar offspring. |
| 177 | Shory aeromancers establish Kho as the first flying city. |
| 513 | The empire of Xa Hoi is founded. |
| 1503 | Yixing forges the Ivory Accord with Nagajor, establishing peace and open trade between humanity and the nagaji. |
| 1868 | The tarrasque destroys the city of Kho. Envisioning a swift end to the empire of the Shory in the chaos that descended in the wake of this disaster, the Shory city of Yjae elects to abandon the nation and flees east over the Obari Ocean. |
| 1869 | The flying city of Yjae makes its fateful attempt at passing over the Wall of Heaven, suffers irreparable damage, and becomes stranded high above the deserts of Shaguang. |
| 2105 | An army of haunted clockwork soldiers emerges from the Clicking Caverns to assault both Nagajor and Xa Hoi. |
| 2456 | A strange object falls from the sky, plummeting into the jungles of Valashmai. Its landing site, known today as the Star Titan's Grave, has yet to be found. |
| 2600 | Shizuru bestows her grace upon five mortal lines, creating imperial families who could eventually come to rule Minkai as emperors. |
| 2612 | The Teikoku Shogunate establishes what is known today as the First Kingdom of Minkai. |
| 2790 | The samurai Zaokoyu and his kingdom are destroyed by the kami of the Forest of Spirits. This land is forevermore regarded as the northern limit to Teikoku's (and later, Minkai's) northern expansion. |
| 2802 | Soong Bai, a brilliant but eccentric hermit, reveals the secrets of acupuncture to Yixing when he saves the life of an explorer who had been grievously wounded by a diseased boar. When word spreads, Yixing seeks to establish a presence in the area, founding the province of Chu Ye. |
| 2813 | Goka is founded by Xhai Xen Xiao, a brilliant architect and priest of Abadar whose conflicts with his superiors in Imperial Yixing forced him to flee the empire. |
| 2826 | Word of the "City of Wonders" being built by Xhai Xen Xiao finally catches the attention of Empress Yin. Against the wishes of her advisors (who desired to annex Goka and imprison Xhai Xen Xiao for having the audacity to build such an impressive city outside of Yixing), she travels to Goka and falls in love with the city's free spirit and breathtaking skyline. Instead of condemning the city, she grants it independent status outside of the empire's normal hierarchy in order to allow Xhai Xen Xiao and his followers the freedom to complete the city's construction as they wish. |
| 2829 | Xhai Xen Xiao dies after a fall from the recently completed first spire of the Seven Dragon Bridge. Rumors of the involvement of yellow-robed assassins in the employ of certain high-placed officials in Yixing fly furiously, but no hard evidence of foul play in Xiao's death ever surfaces. |
| 2970 | General Ishanda Aiko leads a regiment into the throat of Mount Kumiginja and becomes the first to successfully navigate the Ghost Path, although she is forced to abandon all of her soldiers in the outskirts of Shirogoku in order to return to her lord and make her grim report of the strange discoveries within the exposed Sekaminan cavern. |
| 3020 | Yixing officially encompasses the width of Tian Xia. |
| 3089 | The city-state of Bachuan is established by Yixing merchants in an attempt to control trade into Xidao. |
| 3800 | Amatatsu Aganhei establishes the trade route known as the Path of Aganhei between Tian Xia and Avistan over the Crown of the World. Scandalized by this new method of connection to barbaric lands, the shogun of Teikoku orders the explorer executed and destroys what he thinks are all of Aganhei's maps—but the explorer had feared this might happen and stashed copies his maps and notes somewhere safe. Those copies—and the path itself—would remain hidden for 3,000 years. |
| 3808 | A Yixing junk, the *Resplendent Phoenix*, docks in Absalom, representing the first significant contact between Tian Xia and the Inner Sea region. |
| 3810 | Trade with the west is opened in Goka, ushering in a new era of prosperity to the already legendary city. |
| 4687 | The teachings of Irori reach mainland Tian Xia. |
| 5164 | Yixing courtiers perform the first xhadao tea ceremony for their emperor. |
| 5576 | The empire of Yixing collapses. |
| 5580 | The city-state of Bachuan seizes control of the southern Benchu Bay region and swiftly expands into nearby provinces abandoned by Yixing. |
| 5589 | With the fall of Yixing, the Tian-Hwans of the southern lands seize destiny and establish Hwanggot, the Kingdom of Flowers. After extensive study of Yixing focusing on the factors that caused the empire's fall, the leaders of Hwanggot establish their nation with wisdom and pride. |
| 5601 | The empire of Shu is founded. |
| 5723 | Dtang Ma is founded by five sisters, each of whom gained her sorcerous power from a different bloodline. The traditions these five sisters establish persist in Dtang Ma to the present day. |
| 6116 | The Perfect Swordswoman, Setsuna Kuga, leads the armies of the Minkai against the forces of the Teikoku Shogunate at the Battle of Eight Bridges. With the |

shogun's forces routed, Minkai's armies march upon the old capital and raze it.

| | |
|---|---|
| 6119 | The empire of Minkai is established in Tian Xia. Kasai is named the new capital. |
| 6191 | Minkai explorers make contact with Jinin; impressed with the unusually honorable, courteous, and powerful samurai, Jinin becomes a shogunate. |
| 6536 | The empire of Shu collapses. |
| 6642 | Imperial Lung Wa is established in Tian Xia, uniting 10 of the 16 Kingdoms of Shu. |
| 6751 | A rat uprising from the underground realm Diguo-Dashu plagues central Lung Wa. The ratfolk seize control of a dozen cities before the Imperial Army breaks the invading forces and drives them back into Sekamina, sealing no less than 20 known entrances into the Darklands with powerful earth magic. |
| 6780 | Lung Wa founds the province of Kwanlai as a territory for tengus, but does not offer any support for the new nation. Instead, Kwanlai is increasingly treated as little more than a prison colony. |
| 6800 | The lost maps of Aganhei's route over the Crown of the World is rediscovered by another Minkai explorer, and the trade route soon becomes quite well used. |
| 6802 | Lung Wa absorbs Bachuan. |
| 6804 | Hwanggot surrenders to Lung Wa when it becomes apparent that a diplomatic route to Hwanggot's continued independence is impossible. |
| 6898 | Construction of the Eternal Emperor begins in Changdo—the enormous statue remains unfinished to this day. |
| 6932 | Lung Wa's first failed attempt to conquer Dtang Ma indirectly results in the death of Lung Wa's emperor. |
| 6980 | The Seven Year War begins between Lung Wa and Dtang Ma. |
| 6987 | The Seven Year War ends with Dtang Ma being conquered by Lung Wa. |
| 7010 | Pham Duc Quan ascends to Xa Hoi's throne. |
| 7059 | The Golden League is founded, and controls Minkai's commerce for 12 years. |
| 7071 | The Golden League is banished from Minkai. |
| 7080 | The Golden League resurfaces in Goka. |
| 7099 | Mount Pho-Yim explodes, devastating Dtang Ma. The eruption is unofficially blamed on Lung Wa's conquest of the nation. |

## AGE OF SUCCESSION

| Date | Event |
|---|---|
| 7106 | Aroden dies. Lung Wa collapses. The government of Lung Wa falls apart, splitting into religious, military, and traditional factions. These three factions each settle in different Successor States, and poor relations between these three—Lingshen, Quain, and Po Li—persist to this day. |
| 7107 | The towns and villages of Shenmen fall under the sadistic control of Lady Lang Loi. |
| 7108 | General Orphyrea Amanandar and her army arrives at the city of Kamikobu and defeat a dozen bandit warlords to restore peace to the beleaguered settlement. The city is renamed "New Oppara." |
| 7109 | Several embittered Lung Wa ship captains begin construction of the floating pirate city of Zo Piaobo. |
| 7110 | The hobgoblins of Kaoling seize control of six squabbling states between Jinin and Shaguang, proclaiming the captured lands theirs. |
| 7111 | Storms wrack Wanshou until the nation's misguided prayers result in their dubious salvation by an elder kraken named Zhanagorr. |
| 7113 | Oni take control of Chu Ye. |
| 7119 | Sulunai single-handedly brings about Tianjing's salvation, uniting the aasimars against the bandits and worse who sought to plunder the nation's riches. |
| 7120 | The Gunworks of Alkenstar are completed. The earliest firearms begin to emerge from Alkenstar—and the first such imports reach Tian Xia only 7 months later. Almost immediately, Goka puts extensive restrictions on the import of the weapons. |
| 7151 | The oni known as the Five Storms launch their plan to take control of Minkai by escaping the House of Withered Blossoms in the Forest of Spirits. |
| 7152 | The oni complete the destruction or stealthy subjugation of four of the five royal families of Minkai, leaving the Amatatsu family as the last holdout. Yet when the oni turn their attention to this family, they discover that the Amatatsus have fled Minkai over the Crown of the World. |
| 7168 | Grandfather Pei dies; rule of Bachuan passes to his not-nearly-so-friendly wife. |
| 7176 | Toriaka, the man destined to become the Sun Shogun of Shokuro, is exiled from Minkai. Eager to put his shame behind him, he seeks out the legendary elves of Jinin, only to become embroiled in the atrocities afflicting northeastern Lingshen. |
| 7199 | Burning Cloud Devil, the self-proclaimed King of Heroes, disrupts the ceremony of the Celestial Dragon, ushering in 12 years of drought and other peril to the Successor State of Quain. |
| 7208 | Zethivaxus Djeed, a nagaji hero, goes missing after an ill-advised expedition into the Clicking Caverns. He emerges 9 months later—but in the body of a clockwork abomination at the head of an army of ravenous haunted clockworks bent on destroying and harvesting highland villagers from western Xa Hoi. |
| 7210 | An increase in the number of unexplained sinkings among trade vessels sailing the waters of Xidao strains relations between Minkai and the locathah. |
| 7211 | The current year. |

## AMANANDAR

### Western Empire in the East

**Alignment:** LN

**Capital:** New Oppara
(20,154)

**Notable Settlements:**
Funako (18,893), Okim
(12,645), Toduc Wa (35,721),
Vannisaria (11,583)

**Ruler:** General Audrya Vannisar
(LN female Taldan fighter 12)

**Government:** Military monarchy

**Major Races:** Taldans, Tian-Shus (also elves, samsarans,
and tengus)

**Languages:** Taldan, Tien

**Religion:** Abadar, Irori, Pharasma, Shizuru

**Resources:** Grain, iron, livestock, mercenaries, western
armor, western weapons, wool

In the waning days of the Age of Enthronement, the western nation of Taldor began to decline. Some believed that the cause of the empire's troubles was linked fundamentally to the fact that Taldor had ceased to grow. The loss of land to war and secession was but a symptom of the empire's loss of interest in expansion, and so a dynamic and young general, one Orphyrea Amanandar, organized a daring solution to the problem—an Eighth Army of Exploration.

General Amanandar set sail from Taldor, planning on finding a new land to rule on the far side of the world, only a few months before Aroden's death threw the Inner Sea region into chaos. Undaunted, she sailed through horrific storms and monster-haunted oceans, and navigated the dangerous waters of the Valashmai Sea between Valashmai and Sarusan—a feat that many naval commanders would be proud of. Yet Orphyrea was only getting started. She sailed up the eastern coast of Tian Xia to find the land entangled in war—the fall of Imperial Lung Wa had left the mainland in chaos as countless Successor States and recently freed thrall nations fought for dominance. The general sailed her fleet between Bachuan and Tianjing, navigated the Sea of Ghosts, and finally made landfall in northern Shenmen. Her ships barely seaworthy, she led her bedraggled army north along the banks of the Gan-Tzou River, seizing territories and destroying enemies, until at last they reached the war-torn city of Kamikobu in the southern foothills of Zi Ha.

Kamikobu had been a major trade city along one of Lung Wa's more important trade routes to the east, a way station for travelers and a central meeting place for the governors of the provinces. When Lung Wa collapsed, the corrupt Tian-Shu government of Kamikobu abandoned the city, fleeing east into what they hoped would be the safety of backwater Wanshou. The numerous bandit lords who dwelled in southern Zi Ha and northern Shenmen had long regarded Kamikobu as a breadbasket, and they spared no energy in attempting to seize this important city for themselves. The citizens of Kamikobu had been caught between a dozen different bickering warlords for well over a year when General Amanandar's troops arrived. Travel-weary as the Taldans were, they (with the aid of Kamikobu's beleaguered citizens) nonetheless managed to defeat the bandits and restore peace to the city.

After the city was won, Orphyrea Amanandar gladly accepted the governor's seat and set about remaking Kamikobu and its environs into a nation-state that would be familiar to her people, beginning by renaming the city to New Oppara and the land itself after her own family name. By the time she died, this nation had become a full-fledged Successor State of its own—and its influence has only continued to grow ever since.

The rule of Amanandar depends not on heredity, but upon military power—the ruler of Amanandar is also the commander of the nation's army. When the nation's leader dies, rule passes to the next-in-command of the army—this position is open only to Taldans. The General of Amanandar is aided by a council of advisors known as the General Staff. All citizens must serve in the military a minimum of 5 years of their lives between the ages of 16 and 45 (the years need not necessarily be contiguous). Because of this, all citizens keep weapons in their homes and drill regularly. Their familiarity with weaponry means that Amanandarans can often find employment as mercenaries and guards for the many caravans that once more roll through on the trade routes.

**Daigaki Castle:** Of the twelve bandit warlords that bickered over the city of Kamikobu during the first few years of the Age of Succession, the most feared was Tsubokandu, a cruel samurai who chose exile from Shokuro rather than honorable seppuku when proof of his treachery in that nation came to light. Rumor holds that after Tsubokandu was defeated by General Amanandar, his ghost returned to this remote castle in the foothills of the Gossamer Mountains, where he works to raise a new army of the dead.

**New Oppara:** The capital city has a relatively strict cap on growth, by order of the General Staff, who do not wish to hamper the city's defenses by constantly building new walls or other defenses. Application to live in the city is a lengthy process and residency is granted to few. This increasingly breeds a sense of entitlement among those who live in New Oppara, with bitterness and jealousy slowly growing among the citizens of the nation's southern cities, all of whom are growing rapidly as word of Amanandar's wealth and success spreads throughout the Successor States.

# BACHUAN

## Children of the Revolution

**Alignment:** LN
**Capital:** Peijia (50,800)
**Notable Settlements:**
Gowbei (39,475), Li
Dowloon (27,200), Naijing (11,450)
**Ruler:** Grandmother Pei (LE old female Tian-Shu
monk 13)
**Government:** Communist dictatorship
**Major Races:** Tian-Shus
**Languages:** Tien
**Religion:** None (religion is suppressed)
**Resources:** Gems, grain, copper, seafood, stone

With the collapse of the unifying authority of the empire of Lung Wa, the greedy, venal officials governing what was once Pen Wa Province did their best to maintain control of the peasant population they had squeezed with impunity for centuries. But a peasant-philosopher who came to be known as Grandfather Pei taught the comradeship of all humanoids, persuading a growing army of followers that their fat, avaricious rulers and the corrupt clergy that supported their abuse of power had no real authority to rule over them now that Lung Wa was no more. Impoverished farmers, brutalized workers in the deep mines and quarries of the rocky Szaezan Crags, and demoralized fisherfolk on Benchu Bay flocked to his banner: a yellow sun on a blue background, around which a tiger (the indigenous people) chased a dragon (the oppressive government). In time the government and their puppet religionists were thrown down, and the Republic of Bachuan (an ancient, pre-Lung Wa name for the region) emerged.

Grandfather Pei's governing philosophy was, in theory, meant to correct the suffering caused by the arbitrary whims and gluttonous appetites of the bloated Lung Wa aristocracy. Theoretically, all people were equal and shared uniformly in both the labor and the fruits of that labor. The state owned all property, directed production and distribution of wealth, and outlawed the practice of any religion, seeing it as a tool of the discredited imperialist overlords. Grandfather Pei led the governing council known as the Sun Chamber until he passed peacefully in his sleep at the age of 101.

Some grumbled about the increasingly autocratic nature of Grandfather Pei's leadership and the grim ideological purges during the last few years of his life, but the most astute instead blamed the gradual shift away from Pei's ideas on the subtle machinations of his sixth wife. Married to Grandfather at the age of 16, she was the only daughter of a family who survived the strenuous re-education camps established in the early years of the republic. Beautiful Pu Yae Men, known now and forever as Grandmother Pei, charmed the aging chairman of the Sun Chamber. Only 29 years old when Grandfather died, she quickly established her supremacy over the Sun Chamber by outmaneuvering half a dozen councilors twice her age and experience.

Bachuan has developed a zeal for spreading the secular gospel of Grandmother Pei's harsher version of Grandfather's philosophy to surrounding nation states, causing substantial friction with its neighbors. However, the most pronounced hostility is directed towards Hwanggot. Bloodless conflicts and diplomatic entanglements have been occurring with increasing regularity along the hotly contested Shuidao River that forms the border between these two nations, and many predict all-out war in the near future.

**Peijia:** Located on the northern shore of Naikang Bay, the capital city of Peijia is an impressive example of a planned city, a near-perfectly executed metropolis designed to house a population of nearly 200,000. Yet Grandfather Pei's dream of such a massive population never came—just over 50,000 people dwell in Peijia today. While this is still a respectable number, the size of the city means the population is spread thin, and entire districts remain empty, giving new revolutionaries, anarchists, and priests plenty of places to hide.

**Szaezan Crags:** While much of the wealth of the now-deposed Lung Wa imperials was confiscated during the revolution's early years, some hidden caches are thought to still exist in remote areas of the state—particularly in the Szaezan Crags, a region now mostly inhabited by a rising population of ogres. The presence of foreigners is tightly controlled and monitored by the infamous Ministry of Peace and Harmony, but some adventuring types have been permitted to explore suspected sites of such caches. The standard reward for braving the dangers of these vaults is 30% of what adventurers recover, with the rest being impounded by various bureaucrats and agencies.

**Ten Thousand Summer Palace:** During the reign of Lung Wa, this sprawling winter palace was a favored retreat for numerous emperors. When the Bachuan Revolution reached this enormous walled compound, its resident sorcerers and priests barred the great palace gates. An entire army of besieging revolutionaries was blasted to ash by the combined power of arcane and divine magic wielded by the palace guards. The gates have not been opened to outsiders since Bachuan's founding, but many have sought a way in. Only one is said to have re-emerged: a Minkai sellsword who stumbled into a nearby village, reeking of sulfur and covered with strange sigils burned into his flesh, clutching an emerald the size of a cabbage. He spoke only two words before dying: "...beautiful...terrible..."

## CHU YE

### Kingdom of the Oni

**Alignment:** LE
**Capital:** Jyito (7,432)
**Notable Settlements:** Kirahata (5,805), Nokkaichi (3,170) Tsukiwa (2,965)
**Ruler:** Shogun Tsuneni (LE male voidlord void yai)
**Government:** Oni shogunate
**Major Races:** Giants, oni (also kitsune, samsaran, Tian-La, Tian-Min, and Tian-Shu slaves)
**Languages:** Giant, Hon-la, Minkaian, Samsaran, Senzar, Tien
**Religion:** Fumeiyoshi, General Susumu
**Resources:** Fish, medicines, and stone

The healers of Chu Ye were particularly well known during the rule of Imperial Lung Wa. Even though they were not generally trusted by Lung Wa's aristocracy (who often derided the notion of seeking out a "farmer's doctor"), the healers of Chu Ye pioneered many methods of nonmagical healing and relaxation, from acupuncture to massage. Yet despite this history of healing, Chu Ye harbored a hideous secret—it was infected by oni.

Capable of assuming humanoid form, the evil spirits known as oni delight in hiding among unsuspecting societies, using the inhabitants to sate their sinister hungers and pleasures. When Lung Wa collapsed, Chu Ye was relatively isolated and protected from direct repercussions of the government's self-destruction, yet it was beset by an even greater evil—the oni that lurked among the populace saw their chance and revealed their true forms. It may have seemed as if every other man, woman, and child threw off their human masks to reveal a demon, but in fact less than 5 percent of Chu Ye's populace were oni. Still, it was enough. The oni seized power, and in the course of a week of bloody horror, the nation went from a kingdom of healing to a kingdom of pain.

For a year, the oni treated Chu Ye as their personal playground, and the nation suffered greatly. Word of the oni's cruelty soon spread, but with chaos and atrocities overwhelming the rest of the continent, none came to save Chu Ye. After a year, a great and powerful oni—a void yai voidlord named Tsuneni—proclaimed himself Shogun of Chu Ye. The nation's violence settled somewhat after that, with giants from the Nightford Mountains and the wildlands of neighboring Zi Ha coming to serve the oni as an army. Although humans still make up a significant a portion of Chu Ye's population, they now form a slave class bound to an oni-scribed doctrine known as the Steel Dictate, a decree that no human may wield a weapon—weapons are for giants and oni alone.

**Chuyokai Forest:** Once feared as a place haunted by monsters, Chuyokai Forest has become, out of necessity, the bastion of the Mizu Ki Hikari, who keep dozens of hidden fortresses along the forest's edge. The deep Chuyokai remains the haunt of monsters to this day—creatures even the oni are hesitant to meddle with. As such, the woods provide an exceptionally strong barrier, preventing conflict with Wanshou to the south.

**Jyito:** Before the fall of Lung Wa, the city of Jyito boasted nearly 30,000 inhabitants. Today, the city is in ruins. It serves now as the Shogunate's throne, a devastation populated by oni, giants, and ogres that must regularly import fresh slaves to replace those killed and eaten.

**VOID YAI ONI**

# DARKLANDS

## Underground Realm of Monsters and Mystery

**Alignment:** CE

**Capital:** None

**Notable Settlements:** Pan Majang (37,900), Rakh Lo (9,200), Shirogoku (22,120)

**Ruler:** None

**Government:** Scattered dictatorships, kingdoms, and theocracies separated by a vast underground wilderness

**Major Races:** Brain oozes, cave giants, denizens of Leng, haunted clockworks, hobgoblins, myceloids, oni, ratfolk, seugathi, troglodytes, underworld dragons

**Languages:** Aklo, Undercommon

**Religion:** Lamashtu, Lao Shu Po, various fiendish demigods

**Resources:** Clockworks, copper, gems, gold, iron, mithral, platinum, silver

The Darklands of Tian Xia are not inhabited by drow and duergar, and no storied "Quest for Sky" saw dwarves drive orcs to the surface in the ancient past. Below Tian Xia, other creatures rule the caves and hidden ways. Yet the fundamental nature of the Darklands remains unchanged—it still consists of three specific "zones"—Nar-Voth, Sekamina, and Orv.

**Well-Known Darklands Entrances:** While entrances to the Darklands can be found throughout Tian Xia, three of them are particularly notorious. The Ghost Path is a series of ledges and caverns that festoon the dormant caldera of the extinguished volcano known as Mount Kumijinja in Minkai's Ikkaku Peninsula—this immense shaft ends in the only region in Sekamina exposed to the light of the sun above. The Clicking Caverns on the border between Xa Hoi and Nagajor are well known to connect to the Darklands, thanks to the periodic armies of strange clockwork warriors that often emerge from the caves to raid both nations. Finally, the elven city of Ayajinbo in Jinin protects a well-defended entrance into the realms below.

**Nar-Voth:** As elsewhere, the caverns of Nar-Voth do not have many significant connections, laterally, to each other—travel from one Nar-Voth complex to another typically requires passage above across the surface or passage below through Sekamina. The haunted caves that surround the caldera of Mount Kumijinja, the clockwork tunnels of the Clicking Caves, and the splendorous Mithral Roots under Jinin are the best-known Nar-Voth complexes to those who dwell on the surface, but a particularly large complex of

fungus-infested caverns dominated by myceloids (*Pathfinder RPG Bestiary 3* 196) and similar horrors is known to those who dwell in Sekamina, for the myceloids often raid into the deeper darkness. Whispers of a second hobgoblin nation ruled by the denizens of the underground city of Rakh Lo persist as well, with reputed entrances leading into Kaoling and Shaguang alike.

**Sekamina:** While the regions of Sekamina below Tian Xia are too numerous to properly catalog in anything other than a book of their own, the simplest approach to these regions focuses on the five most dominant nations found in these twisting caverns. Under much of northern Minkai and the Forest of Spirits lies the spiral-shaped city of Shirogoku—a twisted mockery of the lands above where pallid oni rule over enslaved humans bred like cattle. As might be expected, the deep roots of the Wall of Heaven hide significant caverns as well—many of them inhabited by cave giants (*Bestiary 3* 127), troglodytes, and eerie intrusions from the nightmare realm of Leng. The so-called "Empire of Rats," also known as Diguo-Dashu, sprawls deep under central Tian Xia, where humanoid rats have warred among themselves for ages. Farther south, vast reaches of caverns below the Valashmai Jungle known as Zaikongon are ruled by hideous boneless horrors like seugathi (*Pathfinder RPG Bestiary 2* 243) and brain oozes (*Bestiary 3* 43). Yet perhaps the most unusual and most storied realm in Sekamina is the clockwork necropolis of Pan Majang, deep under Nagajor and Xa Hoi. The source of the strange clockwork inhabitants of this constantly shifting and transforming necropolis is unknown, but the fact that the sadistic, flesh-eating spirits of the forgotten race that built it now possess and haunt the same constructs they once used as slaves has inspired bards and nightmares alike for generations. Pan Majang is ruled by a shadowy council of entities neither undead nor clockwork, yet something horribly in between. Beyond these realms, numerous underworld dragons (*Bestiary 3* 102) such as Kou-Shaguang (whose realm is one of flickering and lambent lights that dance among a maze of dripstones), Zetzubio (who rules a network of caverns also inhabited by blind amphibious oracles), and Geojibom (who takes great pride in sculpting an inverted forest of trees carved from stalactites) are known to often manipulate and orchestrate complex political machinations among the various kingdoms of Sekamina.

**Orv:** Little is known about the vaults of Orv below Tian Xia, although whispers of miniature post-apocalyptic worlds inhabited by malformed giants, oceans of sentient oil that slobbers and gibbers to the creatures that live parasitically in its depths, portals to qlippoth-infested regions of the Abyss, and unknowable monstrosities originally hailing from beyond the Dark Tapestry are recurrent themes among tales of those who claim to have visited these midnight depths.

## DTANG MA

### Feudal Kingdom of Sorcerers

**Alignment:** N
**Capital:** Ramparassad (75,350)
**Notable Settlements:** Duang Kanthir (19,675), Khang Kaw (29,230), Nang Mae (21,200), Phi Seum (25,400)
**Ruler:** Kamraten Khemkhaeng, Wise Tiger Lord of Ramparassad (N male Tian-Dtang sorcerer 11)
**Government:** Feudal confederacy
**Major Races:** Tian-Dtangs
**Languages:** Dtang, Nagaji, Tien
**Religion:** Hei Feng, Nalinivati, Pharasma, Yamatsumi
**Resources:** Alchemical goods, darkwood, dyes, perfume, seafood, songbirds, spices, timber

For many years Lung Wa coveted the lush jungle forests of Dtang Ma, a land renowned for its exotic birds, fine timber, rare spices, and natural perfumes. The empire was foiled time and time again by Dtang Ma's powerful sorcerers, but these defeats only further inflamed Lung Wa's desires to control the idyllic nation. Eventually, after a particularly devastating war that lasted 7 years and cost Lung Wa dearly, the nation of Dtang Ma was conquered, and thereafter its proud people played a subservient role to their conquerors, wary of further angering their oppressors and content to wait out this unfortunate turn of events. As it happened, they had to wait only 2 decades. Dtang Ma reclaimed its independence with Lung Wa's fall, yet it has still not fully recovered from the overwhelming defeat so many centuries ago, and only recently have members of the four sacred bloodlines risen to power enough to rule once again.

The strange feudal confederacy that rules Dtang Ma now is the same that ruled the land for well over a thousand years before it fell to Lung Wa. This confederacy is closely tied to four traditions of sorcerous power—magic from storms, magic from the fey, magic from music, and magic from the stars themselves, with a fifth supreme lord (*kamraten*) sitting on the *Cinnamon Throne* in the capital of Ramparassad, to whom the others owe unquestioned fealty. The *Cinnamon Throne* itself grants the kamraten unique powers, effectively combining the four bloodlines into a fifth complex crossblooded line. These five lords of surpassing prowess assume their offices together, selected via a complex process that takes place in the catacombs beneath the royal palace in Ramparassad. Every 10 years, one of the provincial lords ascends the *Cinnamon Throne*, while the former kamraten joins the three other lords in governing a single province. This eccentric succession continues until one member of the Five dies, whereupon the surviving lords work together to select a replacement from Dtang Ma's most powerful sorcerers.

The rulers now governing Dtang Ma today are the Lord of Bats (stormborn bloodline), Lady of Flowers (fey bloodline), Walker of the Autumn Moon (starsoul bloodline), and Sister Minivet (maestro bloodline). The current kamraten, formerly known as the Tiger Prince, has held the throne for only 2 years. He followed the unprecedented 11-year rule of Tok Wayra, now the Lord of Bats, who managed to avoid relinquishing his hold on the throne for a full year through political maneuvering and underhanded manipulation that scandalized the nation.

**Ramparassad:** The traditional seat of Dtang Ma's kamraten, Ramparassad is also the nation's largest city. Situated at the foot of the volcano Pho-Yim, Ramparassad's distance from the coast has done little to dilute its importance to trade and politics. The stability of the government has always depended on strict adherence to Dtang Ma's unwritten constitution and the mutual dependence of the lords it fosters, for ancient legend holds that it is the harmony of the Five that shields sprawling Ramparassad from devastation from the looming threat of ominously smoking Mount Pho-Yim.

**Sikhyeu Rainforest:** The Dtang Ma interior is dominated by the Sikhyeu Rainforest, a fragrant home of rare avian life, flowers, spices, and other substances greedily sought by alchemists and healers. Many travel the region via the extensive network of rivers and ancient aqueducts and canals built centuries ago by past sorcerer lords, but these waterways pierce what is still in many ways an untamed wild. Outside the feudal capitals of the four provinces, settlements tend to be small hamlets found at regular intervals along the watery highways. Each rural community owes fealty to a local baron, who in turn answers to a provincial lord. The local barons are responsible for collecting taxes and tributes, adjudicating disputes, and keeping the peace. The unsettled majority of the rainforest hides the crumbling temples of strange and forgotten deities, all but swallowed by the jungle. The origin of these forbidding places is a mystery, for no one has been able to decipher the outlandish pictograms covering the walls nor name the grotesque stone idols found within. That these pictograms resist magical translation and seem to change shape upon subsequent visits both confounds and intrigues researchers. These places are common destinations for adventurers, who set out to brave the accursed sites for their reputed riches. Intrepid explorers also hunt the unruly jungle for undiscovered species, substances, and rare plants, all of which fetch astronomical bounties across the continent. The rainforest is infamous, however, for its reclusive maemas—solitary witches who live their strange lives in the deepest jungle, avoiding all humanoid contact.

## FOREST OF SPIRITS

**Sprawling Supernatural Wilderness**

**Alignment:** N
**Capital:** None
**Notable Settlements:** None
**Ruler:** None
**Government:** None
**Major Races:** Fey, kami, kitsune, oni
**Languages:** Senzar, Tien
**Religion:** Daikitsu, Desna, Fumeiyoshi, Sun Wukong
**Resources:** Darkwood, furs, seafood, timber

This vast forest just south of the arctic circle is the primeval birthplace of the kami—spirits who protect those animals, plants, objects, and locations that can't protect themselves against civilization's advance. Since the gods first created the kami, these spirits have spread throughout all of Tian Xia, and in some cases have even begun to spread into other lands beyond the Dragon Empires. They have even started to accept and protect artificial creations as their wards—anything that lacks its own sense of free will and self-awareness might have a kami protector.

But despite the spread of kami throughout the land, it is here in the Forest of Spirits that their power remains the strongest. Not entirely hostile to humanity, the kami are nevertheless wary of letting civilization encroach. But not all of the forest's denizens are so impartial to civilization. Some, such as small settlements of kitsune, manage the delicate balance of being welcoming to outlanders while still honoring the kami's wishes. Others, like forest dragons, the unquiet dead, and corrupted kami who have died only to be reborn as oni dwell in small pockets of woodland where the kami's rule fails. These creatures openly disrespect the kami and work to murder or otherwise bring harm to humanity. The kami suffer these taints within the forest only as long as their depredations do not encroach upon the parts of the forest protected by the kami themselves.

As one approaches the southern coastline, the woods grow thin and small human settlements can be found. A well-traveled route called the Spirit Road hugs this coastline, connecting the nations of Hongal and Minkai—since this route is one of the most important trade routes in all of Minkai, that nation takes great pains to keep it well maintained and to keep the kami satisfied with offerings placed at numerous shrines along the roadside.

The citizens who reside in the small settlements that dot the Spirit Road strike bargains and pacts with the kami, allowing loggers, hunters, fishers, and the like the honor of gathering timber and furs from specifically selected regions along the woodland's edge, provided the people are respectful of the resources. Those who foolishly abuse the honor have a tendency to vanish in the woods. Many speak of the story of the lost empire of Zao in this regard—a kingdom supposedly ruled by a samurai named Zaokoyu. This man was greedy, and demanded more and more timber with which to expand his army and his empire, but as the forest dwindled, the kami grew angry. They rose up against Zaokoyu, recruiting their kin and darker, more dangerous spirits like fey and even a mighty forest dragon to destroy the empire and obliterate all trace of it save for this story, which the kami allowed to survive only to warn future would-be abusers of the Forest of Spirits.

Although much of the Forest of Spirits is protected by the kami, there are places where even these protective creatures dare not tread. One such site is the House of Withered Blossoms, an immense pagoda that once served as both a prison and a palace for a particularly powerful group of oni.

KAMI

## GOKA

### Gateway to the West

**Alignment:** LN

**Capital:** Goka (300,450)

**Notable Settlements:**
Langkhu (5,970)

**Ruler:** Lady Nai Yan Fei (LN
female Tian-Shu rogue 20)

**Government:** Capitalistic constitutional parliament

**Major Races:** Tians (also humans of other ethnicities,
aasimars, dwarves, elves, gnomes, half-elves, half-
orcs, halflings, kitsune, nagaji, samsarans, tengus,
and wayangs)

**Languages:** Dtang, Hon-La, Hwan, Kelish, Minatan,
Minkaian, Nagaji, Samsaran, Taldane, Tengu, Tien,
Vudrani, Wayang

**Religion:** Abadar, Daikitsu, Fumeiyoshi, Hei Feng, Irori,
Lady Nanbyo, Lamashtu, Lao Shu Po, Pharasma,
Shizuru, Sun Wukong, Tsukiyo, Yaezhing

**Resources:** Alcohol, artwork, books, caravan supplies,
drugs, glass, incense, jewelry, magic items, pearls,
poison, rugs, ship supplies, ships, slaves

Enormous Goka is not only the largest city in the Dragon
Empires, but one of the largest in the world, for geography
is destiny. Situated in the only significant break in the
Wall of Heaven's otherwise impassable shield, the city-
state of Goka is the primary point of trade between Tian
Xia and the continents of Avistan, Casmaron, and Garund.
The city's size may be dwarfed by the looming spectacle
of the Wall of Heaven, yet Goka's skyline presents a
significant competitor to those majestic mountains. The
shimmering towers of the Gokan Palace atop Diamond
Knoll, the looming ziggurat of the Grand Bank of Abadar,
the graceful spires of the Seven Dragon Bridge, and the
awe-inspiring 250-foot-tall statues of Shizuru and Tsukiyo
that guard the entrance to Xu Hong Bay present sights that
few travelers ever forget.

Goka has long been the site of civilization, and for as
long, has been a crown jewel coveted by empires. The city
itself has been part of every significant dynasty to rise in
the Dragon Empires starting with the reign of Empress
Yin of Yixing. The empress's avaricious advisors took her
on a guided tour of Goka, hoping to persuade the young
and sheltered ruler to censure the tumultuous burgeoning
place so that they could then annex it for their own
personal gain. However, Yin fell in love with the city's free
spirit and its wild side of gambling and parties. Instead of
condemning Goka, she defied her court and proclaimed
that the city would continue in perpetuity, granting it
special independent status outside the normal hierarchy

of the empire. Of course, this status ended with the
eventual fall of Yixing, and since then, Goka has endured
an alternating cycle of self-rule and subservience.

Goka weathered the fall of Lung Wa with ease and grace,
just as it had the fall of other empires. Today, the sprawling
city is ruled by Lady Nai Yan Fei, a beloved daughter of the
long-established Gokan aristocracy. Most describe Yan Fei
as a rare prodigy—an eloquent and honorable woman who
is still more than willing to embrace change and strive for
improvement and progress. In any city of Goka's size there
is bound to be unrest, but Yan Fei's ability to mediate and
control disquiet is remarkable.

Gokan citizens are inveterate gamblers; from senior
citizens bunched around complex tile games of tiam jeuk
in cramped, dirty teahouses to nobles attending high-class
drake races with lavish prizes, the people of Goka love to
cheer, wager, and test their luck. Tournaments are common
in the city as well—events where skilled individuals can
combine their itch for gambling with the thrill of direct
competition against other champions. Among the greatest
and most famous of Goka's tournaments is the martial
arts spectacle known as the Ruby Phoenix Tournament.

As with any large city, Goka has its dangerous side.
While trading in drugs, poison, and slaves is legal in Goka,
it is extensively regulated, ensuring a healthy black market
thrives—and thus ensuring that numerous thieves' guilds
have plenty to keep them busy. Evil cults, particularly
those of Lamashtu, Lady Nanbyo, and Fumeiyoshi, are a
constant problem as well. Pickpockets, scam artists, pushy
vendors, swindlers, and swarms of beggars are all plentiful.
Numerous gangs of tattooed criminals who specialize in
muggings and other forms of targeted violence, known
collectively as alley bashers, exist in the city's slums. The
most infamous of the alley bashers are the Dragon Fangs,
a powerful, well-organized group said to have the occult
power to animate their deadly draconic tattoos.

During Goka's 4,000 years, the city has acquired an
extensive network of subterranean chambers known
as Undermarket. The levels of this sprawling substrate
complex stretches under the entire city and its harbor. The
deeper one travels into Undermarket, the more dangerous
it gets, transitioning from black markets and thieves'
guilds in the uppermost levels to forgotten catacombs,
buried vaults, and underground cathedrals claimed by
outlawed cults below. The deepest levels are said to lead
into unworked caverns that link to the Darklands, and tales
of an extensive shadow community called Deepmarket,
populated by bickering ratfolk, dark folk, troglodytes,
wayangs, and worse, are common among adventurers.
Certainly, the city of Goka and its Undermarket offer
enough opportunities for excitement that one can make a
name as a successful adventurer without ever leaving the
city at all.

## HONGAL

### Tundra of the Horse Lords

**Alignment:** N
**Capital:** Ordu-Aganhei (8,227)
**Notable Settlements:** Muliwan (2,250)
**Ruler:** Kiriltai Khan (LN male Tian-La cavalier 15)
**Government:** Khanate of loosely affiliated tribes
**Major Races:** Tian-Las (also giants, kitsune, samsarans, and Tian-Mins)
**Languages:** Hon-La, Minkaian, Senzar, Tien
**Religion:** Abadar, Desna, General Susumu, Irori, Kofusachi, Yamatsumi
**Resources:** Avistani goods, furs, horses, mercenaries

The people of Hongal, the Tian-Las, have never known any rule other than their own. As the northernmost country of the Dragon Empires, Hongal has long been regarded as simply being too far and too remote for annexation by the various empires that have ruled the mainland. Hongal's greatest point of interest to other lands is that the fabled Path of Aganhei, the greatest trade route between Tian Xia and Avistan, begins in its northern reaches. To the people of Hongal, this path and the Spirit Road that connects it to the southern nations are seen as necessary evils—routes to bring valuable trade into and through Hongal. As long as these visiting traders spend their coin and don't deviate too far from the roads, the horse lords suffer their presence, but those who venture too far from the trade route risk attracting the wrong kind of attention, for by traditional agreement, any travelers encountered out of sight of the Spirit Road or the Path of Aganhei are considered the property of the first Tian-La tribe to find them.

With the exception of those few who dwell in the cities, the Tian-Las are a nomadic people. While they often travel in smaller groups, these groups band together to form huge, townlike encampments of anywhere from a few dozen to several thousand people when they halt. Hongal's nomads have strict codes of honor and bravery, and sometimes honor their horses more than their own families.

Each Tian-La tribe is ruled by a *baga bohd* (a title equivalent to duke) whose rule is all for that tribe, yet who must cleave with absolute loyalty to the baga bohds of greater tribes. Most Tian-La tribes also contain a small but powerful cabal of spellcasting elders (traditionally female oracles and sorcerers) who provide magical support and advice to the baga bohd. The greatest tribe of all is traditionally the one ruled by Hongal's khan—the supreme ruler of the Tian-La tribes. Currently, this is Kiriltai Khan, a ruler known for his ferocity in both in appetite and anger, yet whose honeyed tongue is said to be capable of talking a horse out of its skin.

The horse-masters of Hongal are said to be among the best riders in Tian Xia, and Hongali horses are much prized throughout the Dragon Empires. Great horse markets are held frequently throughout the year, and grand prizes are on offer for the fastest, most daring, and most reckless riders. Horses sired by stallions of certain rare bloodlines are sometimes sold for thousands of gold pieces.

Hongal currently boasts only two permanent settlements, with one situated at each end of the nation. To the south lies the town of Muliwan, while to the north, where the Path of Aganhei begins, lies the nation's capital-by-default, Ordu-Aganhei. This is not the Khan's seat of government, however—instead, he travels with a nomadic tent city in a vast circuit across Hongal.

The majority of the rest of Hongal is wilderness, with very few permanent structures that can withstand the region's seemingly endless winds. Of these storms, the most feared is the seasonal *quqotengir* (the "sky dragon's angry breath"), which whips across Hongal every early spring and late fall. Dangerous creatures are believed to use these windstorms to hunt and, at times, even control them. The strangely mutilated corpses left behind after particularly ferocious windstorms seem to support such claims, for no known wind can turn a horse inside out or scour the bones from a human body while leaving the flesh intact.

**Ordu-Aganhei:** Beyond being the city at the start of the Path of Aganhei, and thus the last place traders headed to Avistan can obtain supplies and the first place traders from Avistan visit, Ordu-Aganhei is famed for its thermal hot springs, which have formed a lake in the center of the city. Ordu-Aganhei is ruled by a prince—traditionally one of the brothers of the current khan of Hongal. The city's current ruler, Prince Batsaikhar, is a ferocious enemy of filth and somewhat notorious in Hongal for preferring the comforts of civilization over the travails of nomadic life.

**Ruins of Maiaji:** Once the southernmost of Hongal's cities, Maiaji is now home to a violent tribe of ogres and hill giants led by a brute named Nghiem, a legendarily short-tempered ettin with a fondness for horse flesh. Nghiem, while in theory owing allegiance to Chu Ye, thinks of himself as an emperor, and of Maiaji as his nation—one he hopes to build up to something that might rival the greatest of the Dragon Empires. The cornerstone of his plan is siring an army—at last count, he has over 400 sons (he lost count of his daughters), all of whom seem to share their father's anger and desire to rule. While Kiriltai Khan is aware of this growing threat, he has yet to fully deploy the horse lords against Maiaji, for rumor holds that he would rather send "disposable resources" (adventurers) on such a dangerous mission.

# HWANGGOT

## Kingdom of Flowers

**Alignment:** NG
**Capital:** Haseong (151,650)
**Notable Settlements:**
Cholok (34,430), Hyecho
(18,435), Keundol (27,100),
Maecho (43,540)
**Ruler:** Her Most Transcendent Royal Majesty, Queen
Hyun Eun-suk (NG female Tian-Hwan bard 15)
**Government:** Hereditary monarchy
**Major Races:** Tian-Hwans (also kitsune, tengus, Tian-
Dans, Tian-Dtangs, and Tian-Shus)
**Languages:** Hwan, Tien
**Religion:** Desna, Hei Feng, Kofusachi, Shelyn, Sun
Wukong
**Resources:** Artwork, cloth, clothing, coffee, herbs, honey,
incense, opium, perfume, poultry, silk, sugar, tea

If any land can be regarded as a bastion of peace, that land would be Hwanggot. Through a combination of skilled diplomacy and open arms, the Tian-Hwans have long managed to maintain their independence from external rule. The greatest exception to this was their annexation by Lung Wa—when attempts at diplomacy failed to prevent the imperial machine of Lung Wa from attempting to take over Hwanggot, the leaders ceded control without a fight. That the people of Hwanggot neither rebelled nor held grudges against their leaders for this bloodless surrender strikes many as miraculous in its own right, but to the Tian-Hwans, the prevention of violence by whatever means necessary is hardly a miracle at all—it is merely the responsibility of all things given the gift of life in the first place. Under Lung Wa's rule, resource-rich Hwanggot was plundered for the comfort and delight of distant aristocrats, and the so-called Kingdom of Flowers has only recently managed to work its way back up to its pre-invasion status as one of Tian Xia's greatest producers of artwork, exotic foodstuffs, sweets, tea, and opium.

Many Tian historians have pondered the riddle of how this relatively small nation has been able to defy the might of empires and maintain its traditions and patriotism even under years of external rule, pointing to the amazing loyalty of its people, the cleverness of its defenses, and the skill of its diplomats. While these have all factored into the nation's tenacity, it is the incredibly distinctive culture of Hwanggot and the unity it fosters that should be given credit. The arts are honored in Hwanggot to an extent that far exceeds the honor most other nations place upon their military traditions. Lung Wa propagandists were known to wryly observe that the artistic qualities of an archer's

form are valued more by Hwans than whether she actually strikes her target. But it is the harmonious union of creative endeavor and practical matters that has made the kingdom a bulwark against foreign hegemony.

The current dynasty of Nuri has reigned for the past 2 centuries, navigating the kingdom through Lung Wa's dramatic demise and ushering in an era of increased prosperity. Queen Hyun Eun-suk has ruled Hwanggot for over 50 of those years, and at the age of 78, is in the process of ceding control of the kingdom's defense to her eldest daughter and heir, Princess Hyun Geon-ji. However, as the aged queen slowly recedes into the background, there is some concern that the transition following her inevitable death may not be as smooth as might be hoped, for Princess Geon-ji seems strangely restless and aggressive for a member of that proud family line. Rather than adopt the traditional role of diplomacy against Hwanggot's greatest current enemy, Bachuan, the princess instead ordered the erection of a network of mammoth stone fortresses along the Shuidao River—the border the two countries share. Government agents work night and day to explain and disprove rumors that Hwans have been captured by Bachuan agents who have infiltrated Hwanggot, and that the captives have been tortured or even transformed into undead assassins to be sent back into the Kingdom of Flowers to spread misery.

**Chang Liao Jungle:** While the edges of the Chang Liao Jungle are regularly harvested for lumber, the interior is another matter. Within its deepest places are isolated tribes known collectively as the Sunsu Godae. These isolated Tian-Hwans adhere to Hwanggot's primitive warlike practices of the ancient past. The Sunsu Godae are extraordinarily hostile to outsiders (their reaction to intrusion by other Tian-Hwans is only slightly less hostile than their reaction to encounters with Tian-Shus, and other unwary explorers foolish enough to fall into their hands are known to suffer terrible tortures concocted by a people of startling cruelty. As despised as the Sunsu Godae might be, the people of civilized Hwanggot secretly admire their savage kin, for the Sunsu Godae have long made the depths of the Chang Liao Jungle dangerous for foreign armies to traverse.

**Haseong:** The cosmopolitan port of Haseong is one of Hwanggot's prides and joys. Despite the nation's growing tensions, Haseong remains famous for its many festivals celebrating every art form, painting, song, cuisine, sculpture, dance, theater, poetry, and pottery being the most common. In addition, scores of annual fairs celebrate industry and products, such as the late summer Honey Festival, or the marvelous winter celebration of metal workers that brings people flocking to the waterfront. These distinctive festivals all have their competitions and coveted prizes, and are open to outsiders as well as to Hwans.

## JININ

### Displaced Elven Nation

**Alignment:** LG
**Capital:** Ayajinbo (9,042)
**Notable Settlements:**
  Hevara (7,400) Huilitien (2,270),
  Jinushie (5,120), Kyorasa (3,700), Yinzushan (4,600)
**Ruler:** Shogun Jininsiel Ryuikiatsu of the Bamboo Court
  of Silver Leaves (LG male elf samurai 15)
**Government:** Shogunate
**Major Races:** Elves (also some half-elves, samsarans,
  Taldans, and Tian-Mins)
**Languages:** Elven, Samsaran, Tien
**Religion:** Desna, Qi Zhong, Shelyn, Shizuru, Tsukiyo
**Resources:** Artwork, bamboo, fruit, magic items,
  mithral, silver

After the devastation of the Earthfall, many of the elves of the Mierani Forest in Varisia chose not to leave Golarion through the gates to Sovyrian. Instead, they fled into the darkness of Nar-Voth, going deeper to find shelter in Sekamina. It was upon reaching this level of the Darklands that an elven oracle named Jininsiel experienced an overwhelming vision of a silver tree—she knew that salvation for her people could be found by seeking the roots of this tree and following them up, and where they emerged they would find a new land where they could start their lives anew. Yet the majority of the elves believed that salvation lay in going ever deeper, resulting in a painful schism when Jininsiel and several hundred of her closest friends and followers were forced to depart from the main elven host—they were even denied a fair share of the food and supplies by the increasingly covetous elves who wished to seek shelter ever deeper.

Jininsiel and her generation would never learn of the dire fate that awaited those they left behind—they instead set out to wander the labyrinthine and seemingly endless tunnels of Sekamina for hundreds of years, taking their steps slowly and cautiously, often stopping to hole up in a sheltered cavern to simply outlive larger settlements of monsters and creatures they found blocking their way. Eventually, they came upon a shockingly vast mithral lode that resembled nothing so much as the immense roots of a silver tree. Following the mithral veins upward, the elves emerged after centuries in the dark into a new land—the heart of Tian Xia. Jininsiel died a few weeks later, content that her vision had led her kin to safety, and they named the idyllic forest realm they now found themselves in after her—the nation of Jinin has remained one of Tian Xia's oldest and most mysterious kingdoms ever since.

Today, the elves of Jinin have adopted the lifestyles of honor and duty that bind the samurai of Minkai, inspired by Tian-Min visitors a thousand years before (tales of these same travelers would eventually inspire the first Sun Shogun to travel to central Tian Xia, where he founded Shokuro). They are more ordered and respectful of tradition than are the elves of the distant west, and upon learning of the fate that eventually transformed their kin into drow so long ago, have only further embraced the virtues of law and personal honor. They guard well the secret entrance to the Mithral Roots, the caverns where they carefully mine just enough mithral to keep their people in comfort via trade—visitors to Jinin are respectfully welcomed, but not encouraged to linger.

**Ayajinbo:** The elves of Jinin are not as numerous as the inhabitants of other countries, but Jinin's capital city of Ayajinbo remains one of the Dragon Empires' great hidden treasures. Many have traveled to Ayajinbo merely to meditate for an hour in one of its silvered gardens, and admire its towers of stone decorated with delicate mithral and crystalline designs. The heart of the city guards the same entrance to the Darklands that the elves used to emerge into Tian Xia so long ago. Very few outlanders have had the honor of following the mithral roots into these chambers, but the caverns are said to be among the most beautiful locations in all the Dragon Empires. Certainly, they are one of the continent's richest resources, and mithral from Jinin is a valued export.

**SHOGUN JININSIEL RYUIKIATSU**

# KAOLING

## Brutal Hobgoblin Empire

**Alignment:** LE
**Capital:** Dhucharg (24,550)
**Notable Settlements:** Gajang (10,100),
 Homgul Hills (17,300), Hyeolsha
 (9,800), Jalli (5,700)
**Ruler:** Warlord Tsung-cha Kavangaki (LE
 male hobgoblin fighter 4/samurai 12)
**Government:** Military dictatorship
 officiated by a council of nine warlords
**Major Races:** Hobgoblins (also ettins,
 hill giants, and ogres, as well as many
 human, elven, and samsaran slaves)
**Languages:** Giant, Goblinoid
**Religion:** General Susumu, Yaezhing
**Resources:** Armor, iron, leather goods,
 livestock, slaves, weapons

When the lands of Kaoling were part of Lung Wa, the hobgoblins of the northern hills were an ever-present threat. As quickly as one tribe and its warlord were put down, a new warlord seemed to rise from the apparently endless hobgoblin rabble to begin raiding farms and villages anew. Regardless of the number of soldiers Lung Wa hurled at the hobgoblin menace, they seemed without number. So it was for centuries, until Lung Wa fell and the empire's troops no longer came. At first, the hobgoblin raids in the northern frontiers were of little concern—a few burned and looted villages. But when no army arrived to oppose them, the hobgoblins realized that things had changed. The next attack on the surrounding lands was the largest the region had yet seen—well-organized, brutal, and, ultimately, unstoppable. In the span of only a few years, no fewer than six bickering would-be Successor States were destroyed by the hobgoblins. For decades, the hobgoblins held the lands between the borders of Shaguang and Jinin, the size and shape of the land's borders resulting as much from the distance hobgoblin armies were willing to travel from their caverns below the Shaguang Rise as from the significant resistance they finally encountered from the elves of Jinin and the armies of Lingshen. In a move that was as wise as it was uncharacteristic of goblinoids, the rulers of the hobgoblin horde decided that what they'd taken was enough and settled in to found a nation—Kaoling.

Following the example of its Lung Wa rivals, Kaoling instituted an extensive bureaucracy, answering to the military leadership. Captured enemy leaders were put to death in well-attended public executions, whereas captured humans and others were offered the opportunity to live under their new overlords as slaves, provided they obeyed without question. Lawbreaking for a non-hobgoblin in Kaoling means mutilation or execution, but the hobgoblins also make sure to reward those who cooperate with increased power over their own kind, appealing to the basic nature of human bullying.

A Council of Generals, also known as the Council of Nine, rules Kaoling. The ninth member of the council is chosen from among their number by the other eight to serve as a sort of figurehead leader in the role of warlord. The current holder of the title is Warlord Tsung-cha Kavangaki, a cunning hobgoblin veteran of the latest (and nearly successful) Zi Ha campaign, who built the coalition that ousted his predecessor and currently controls a majority of the council. The warlord casts the tie-breaking vote in all council matters and generally has supreme executive power over the bureaucracy, although in practical terms the council members care little about the day-to-day affairs of state, so long as they are running smoothly.

Kaoling's bureaucrats help to keep order by maintaining exacting records. All hobgoblins are expected to serve in the military, while all slaves must bear proper identification at all times—the use of brands and tattoos makes such identification difficult to lose or hide. Visitors on legitimate business in Kaoling are issued travel papers for the duration of their expected stay, but are watched closely. Those unable to produce documentation are subject to arrest, interrogation, and possibly enslavement or execution. Naturally, there is a brisk business in bribes and false paperwork among the bureaucracy, although it is a dangerous affair, as such crimes expose the bureaucrats to the potential of arrest and execution themselves.

**Dhucharg:** While many of Kaoling's towns are little more than slave camps run by merciless hobgoblin overseers, Dhucharg honestly approaches the status of a proper city capable of receiving visitors and honest trade. The capital's slave-powered foundries and forges constantly turn out armor and weaponry for Kaoling's troops, with the excess being set aside for trade to those who do not see Kaoling as an actual enemy (mostly the Tian-La tribes of Shaguang and Hongal, but also certain Gokan mercantile companies who have made a specialty of smuggling the actually quite well-made hobgoblin arms and armor through Lingshen for sale to the rest of the world).

**Spiritscar:** The Spiritscar is a rift in the northern hills where once a large monastery of Lady Nanbyo was located. Spiritscar was a frightful place in the time of Lung Wa, as the monastery's cultists triggered earthquakes when the hobgoblins attempted to capture the site early in Kaoling's foundational years. In the resulting devastation, the monastery and an entire army of hobgoblins sank into an 800-foot-deep, 7-mile-long rift—the location today remains haunted by the ghosts of hobgoblins and cultists alike.

## KWANLAI

### Rising Tengu Nation

**Alignment:** CN

**Capital:** Hisuikarasu
(19,230)

**Notable Settlements:**
Nagaiyamatsu (7,200),
Seidoyaji (11,300),
Todorokaze (9,440)

**Ruler:** Lady Sutarai-Gongen (CG female half-celestial tengu cleric 14 of Hei Feng)

**Government:** Clan confederation united under a benevolent autocrat

**Major Races:** Tengus (also aasimars, kitsune, locathahs, Tian-Mins, and Tian-Shus)

**Languages:** Minkaian, Tengu, Tien

**Religion:** Desna, Hei Feng, Lao Shu Po, Sun Wukong

**Resources:** Alcohol, coffee, copper, gold, iron, jewelry, salt, seafood, stone, tobacco

Long oppressed by the might of Lung Wa, the tengus of Kwanlai suffered centuries of discrimination outside of their homeland from imperial forces and attitudes that classified them as a race of cowards and thieves. Largely bottled in an underdeveloped corner of the empire and suffocated by taxes, most tengus grew up in the squalor of the nation's few ports and the trade cities along its borders, packed into wood and paper tenements, almost predetermined to become the stereotype they suffered under. That changed 105 years ago during the Feather and Starlight Rebellion, when an army of rogues and priests of Hei Feng and Desna captured and forced the abdication of Lord Som Heu Wa in the final days of Lung Wa's rule—had that empire not collapsed later that same year, Kwanlai would have suffered greatly for this uprising.

For all its peoples' hopes, Kwanlai remains for the moment a true nation on paper only, with its society fractured along the multiple fault lines of historical clan blood-allegiances, religion, and fear of the return to outside rule. Since the fall of Lung Wa, the nation has seen no fewer than three clan wars and the Autumn of Iron Tears, a proxy clan conflict between rival thieves guilds in Seidoyaji and Todorokaze.

Yet for all the tengus' bloody, petty rivalries, the perpetual threat of foreign domination has always kept them united, albeit in a loose fashion. With the rise in power of beloved Lady Sutarai-Gongen in the city of Hisuikarasu, Kwanlai seems poised to finally make the transition between region and nation. Somewhere between revered spiritual leader and outright queen, the half-celestial cleric of Desna has the tacit allegiance of

all five major tengu clans, though the adherents of other gods—especially Lao Shu Po—resent the prominence and swell in worshipers it has given to her faith.

The greatest uniting force in Kwanlai, however, is the nation of Wanshou. Having faced two major invasions from this swampland in the past century, the only thing resembling an organized standing army in Kwanlai watches this northern border. A series of forts, stone and sod walls, and artificially drained swamplands prevents easy transit for Wanshou's waterlogged forces, but it is only a matter of time before the tengus face a significant invasion from the north once again.

Kwanlai is on much better footing with its other neighbors. The tengus maintain heavy trade and good relations with Xidao, sharing a mutual enemy in the kraken overlord of Wanshou. They also have good relations with Tianjing, with ongoing exchanges of clerics, artists, and scholars on a 5-year basis, hoping to mutually benefit both nations, as both suffered greatly in recent years. Kwanlai also has an uncertain and evolving relationship with Amanandar, complicated by the expansionist ethos of the original Taldan armies and the memories of the human immigrants to Kwanlai, which give rise to mutual distrust despite the open-minded and benevolent rule of their current queen.

**City of Whistling Swords:** Lost in the high eastern foothills of Kwanlai, the abandoned ruins of the region's old, pre-Lung Wa capital city waits to be rediscovered. Though the ruins are largely forgotten by the tengus, many outsiders seek to return and reclaim the City of Whistling Swords—if only to regain the weapons said to lie hidden still in the city's armories. Unfortunately, the city has become infested with ratfolk, oni, and other evil spirits and monsters, said to be led by a bitter underworld dragon forced out of his home to live in exile on the surface.

**Hisuikarasu:** Most of Kwanlai's cities are located along its coast, and most of them are sprawling slums with little or no sense of urban planning. Not so in the case of the nation's capital city of Hisuikarasu. Here, the tengus have bowed to the guidance of a beloved new leader, the half-celestial Lady Sutarai-Gongen. Under her rule, Hisuikarasu is growing quickly as the country comes to grips with its identity and the long, hard process of uplifting itself from its own squalor.

**Vale of Green Spears:** Located in south central Kwanlai stands an incredibly dense forest of towering bamboo the size of redwoods within a long, narrow valley, grown by the result of a wizard's experiment a thousand years earlier. The vale is said to be the lair of a titanic forest dragon who plundered dozens of merchant ships in the Xidao Gulf, but little of the legendary wyrm has been seen of late. In truth, the dragon died, but her final clutch of eggs survived and her young offspring now lurk among the bamboo.

## LINGSHEN

### Empire of Eternal Armies

**Alignment:** LN
**Capital:** Xiwu (226,000)
**Notable Settlements:** Ahjing
   (61,000), Danjin (95,000),
   Heizhong (133,000)
**Ruler:** King Huang (LN male
   Tian-Shu fighter 20)
**Government:** Hereditary monarchy
**Major Races:** Tian-Shus
**Languages:** Tien
**Religion:** Abadar, Hei Feng, Irori, Yaezhing
**Resources:** Armor, beef, clay, iron, grain, mercenaries,
   pork, pottery, stone, weapons

Mightiest of the Successor States, Lingshen controls the largest armies in part because its finest soldiers never cease to serve. Upon the soldiers' deaths, their spirits inhabit specially crafted terra-cotta warriors. This eternal loyalty is one of the 99 proofs that the succession of Imperial Lung Wa rightfully falls to Lingshen, although Quain and Po Li, Lung Wa's other "true scions," would disagree.

King Huang and his armies offer their foes one chance to surrender. Those who refuse are slain to the last man, woman, and child—even livestock and pets perish, their bodies left to rot as a warning to others. Victims of these ruthless tactics consider King Huang a monster, while others celebrate his goal of unifying the Successor States.

Each of King Huang's sons and daughters commands an army. While their loyalty to their father remains unquestioned, these generals frequently war among themselves. The king tolerates such strife only until it threatens the security of the nation. At that point, he steps in to chastise the one he deems the weaker or more foolish, rewarding the more powerful with land and soldiers.

After warcraft, the most honored skill among nobles in Lingshen is calligraphy. Long before joining the war colleges, the scions of Lingshen attend one of several celebrated writing schools; the rivalry among these schools is the leading cause of duels in Lingshen. There they learn to paint brush strokes approaching aesthetic perfection. The content is unimportant, so one who composes doggerel in beautiful strokes is revered above a brilliant poet with an inelegant hand. It is said that a commander who can write her strategy in the most perfect brush strokes can be assured of victory.

**Battle Forges:** Five sites throughout Lingshen harbor the nation's mighty foundries, where legions of smiths produce the masterwork arms of the country's elite warriors. Also created here are the most advanced siege engines in all of Tian Xia. It is whispered that the royal engineers struck a bargain with several underworld dragons to imbue their creations with supernatural strength.

**Cradle of Immortality:** In the hills far north of the Golden River, royal artisans sculpt the likenesses of Lingshen's greatest warriors into terra-cotta statues. With the blessing of the Underworld Dragon, the royal wizards connect the souls of the warriors to their clay simulacra. When one of these warriors dies, the statue comes to life, allowing the dead soldier to continue serving his lord— at least until the magical statue is destroyed, whereupon the warrior's soul is lost forever.

**Xiwu:** The capital city of Lingshen can seem to a newcomer's eyes to be nothing more than the world's largest military stronghold—and to a certain extent, that impression is correct. The towering castles and fortifications that fill Xiwu's skyline are meant as much to inspire the people of Lingshen as they are to boast of the region's resources and the skill of its architects.

TERRA-COTTA SOLDIER

## MINATA

### The Wandering Isles

**Alignment:** CN
**Capital:** None
**Notable Settlements:** Inahiyi (6,245), Jainai (3,375), Waunomani (5,350), Zo Piaobo (2,310)
**Ruler:** Countless local warlords, captains, chieftains, rulers, and other regional leaders
**Government:** Varies by isle
**Major Races:** Tian-Sings, wayangs
**Languages:** Aquan, Minatan, Tien, Wayang
**Religion:** Desna, Hei Feng, Lady Nanbyo, Lao Shu Po, Sun Wukong, numerous tribal cults
**Resources:** Ambergris, mercenaries, pearls, rope, seafood, ship supplies, ships, slaves, whale oil

Legend has it that when the gods created Golarion, Minata was a single enormous bridge of land that connected Tian Xia with the mysterious southern continent of Sarusan. In those ancient days, a civilization of surpassing magnificence known as Taumata ruled this mythical land bridge, but when its people blasphemed against the gods, Hei Feng descended from the skies in a rage. He cut Minata apart with his mighty nine-ring broadsword, then kicked and scattered the resulting islands across the sea, saying, "Nevermore in unity, lest you think yourselves greater than those who gave you life." Ever since, the islands of Minata have been notoriously difficult to navigate, particularly as one sails further south.

Most scholars think of Hei Feng's supposed destruction of the mythical Minatan land bridge as nothing more than a fanciful creation myth. Indeed, the concept that Minata itself was once a land bridge between Tian Xia and Sarusan is often dismissed as fiction—despite the fact that brave explorers periodically return from remote isles in the archipelago with strange archaeological evidence or tales of unusual structures that follow no known Tian architectural styles.

Minata is arguably the most diverse region in all of Tian Xia, with a breathtaking profusion of cultures and peoples. Many of these populations are remarkably isolated despite their short distance from neighboring communities, while other clusters of islands form loose confederacies or pay tribute to a petty monarch.

**Atas Pulu:** This northernmost expanse of islands has been most successfully exploited by the nations of Tian Xia, and these petty kingdoms, some encompassing no more than a single small isle, trade extensively with the mainland. The largest islands in this part of Minata make up the Shibobekas—a series of islands that once formed a single immense volcano named Mount Shibotai. When Mount Shibotai erupted at the end of the Age of Ashes, it blanketed much of Tian Xia in ash—since then, the volcano has been quiet, and its shattered remains have formed a ring-shaped set of islands with particularly fertile soil. These islands are the home of numerous tribes of wayangs who believe that Mount Shibotai's ancient eruption coincided with their race's emergence into Golarion. The isle at the center of this ring is the location of the city of Inahiyi, which is devoted exclusively to the wayangs' appeasement of the demon thought to live still in the flooded volcanic crater.

**Tengah Pulu:** The central and largest expanse of islands is a somewhat wilder region, characterized primarily by mountainous jungles inhabited by tiny groups of primitive tribesmen whose practices, it is believed by mainlanders, include headhunting, cannibalism, and necrophilia. That some of these tribes engage in such activities is without doubt, but though these evil tribes' hideous traditions color all of the people of Tengah Pulu with broad, vile strokes, they are in the minority. The largest island here is known as Belem—a great island famous for its hundreds of hidden coves and treacherous shoals. It is the single largest haven for pirates in Minata. The bustling port town of Waunomani on the island's central eastern coast acts as a capital of sorts, though to suggest any sort of functioning government would elicit laughter from anyone who has visited. While the mysterious wayangs are scattered across the archipelago and are the majority inhabitants of a number of smaller island communities, the hammer-shaped island of Bukorang is exclusively theirs.

**Rendah Pulu:** Without a doubt, this southern stretch of islands is the most feared region of Minata, inhabited by demon-worshiping humanoids, many of whom enthusiastically practice cannibalism. Most notorious are the islands of Lakapuna and Olakapuna, off the coast of the Valashmai Jungle and home to all manner of monstrous horrors, as well as to cloistered priests and sorcerers of vile reputation, practitioners of unspeakable blasphemies. Even pirates avoid this region of Minata, but rumors that the most intact remnants of legendary Taumata can be found in these hostile islands draw new adventurers every year.

**Zo Piaobo:** This strange principality is a literal floating city, comprising hundreds of boats, rafts, and masses of driftwood lashed together to form one huge artificial island. Home to at least 2,000 Tian-Sing souls, it drifts eternally between Atas Pulu and Tengah Pulu. Some natives break off from their floating city and wander throughout coastal Tian Xia, living on little flotillas called kipakus in the harbors and river mouths of many Tian nations. The rulers of this floating city, the Zo, constitute Minata's largest allied fleet of pirates, and their word and influence carry far throughout the Wandering Isles. If any group has a shot at uniting Minata's pirate clans, it is the Zo.

## MINKAI

### Empire of Dawn

**Alignment:** LN
**Capital:** Kasai (164,200)
**Notable Settlements:**
 Akafuto (42,500), Enganoka
 (19,420), Hiyosai (7,290),
 Oda (11,200), Sakakabe
 (23,500), Shogokabe (62,450), Wanshi (11,390)
**Ruler:** The Jade Regent (race and class unknown)
**Government:** Imperial regency served by regional
 governors
**Major Races:** Tian-Mins (also kitsune, tengus, Tian-
 Hwans, Tian-Las, and Tian-Shus)
**Languages:** Minkaian, Tien
**Religion:** Daikitsu, Desna, Fumeiyoshi, General Susumu,
 Hei Feng, Irori, Shelyn, Shizuru, Tsukiyo, Yamatsumi
**Resources:** Alcohol, ambergris, artwork, beef, copper,
 dyes, gold, grain, jade, paper, pearls, seafood, silk,
 silver, tea, timber, vegetables, whale oil

The empire of Minkai could have been the successor to Lung Wa as the dominant nation of the Dragon Empires, for proud Minkai was never fully under the rule of Lung Wa—its independence ensured by its isolation from the mainland and its relatively strong ties to Avistan via the northern trade route known as the Path of Aganhei. When Lung Wa fell, Minkai was largely unaffected—trade with the mainland suffered, but Minkai had always been self-sufficient. The empire didn't immediately move to replace lost Lung Wa, though, for its leaders wisely chose to let the Successor States work out their aggressions. Yet just as Minkai began to expand its influence into the rest of Tian Xia, internal problems like government corruption, peasant rebellions, and increased banditry from the northern barbarian tribes began plaguing the country. Distracted by these growing problems, Minkai never did turn its attention fully to the Successor States, and now, with its emperor missing and an increasingly corrupt Jade Regent ruling from the Imperial Palace in Kasai, the once-mighty empire stands poised on the brink of civil war.

Minkai is, truth be told, no stranger to the horrors of civil war. The nation has endured several during its existence, although to date, none of these wars have fundamentally changed the empire's philosophy or methods of rule. In fact, Minkai has always been ruled by emperors from one of five families invested with the divine right to rule by Shizuru herself. While one ruling family might command for several generations, it has traditionally been but a matter of time before another rose in power to take the previous family's place. Minkai's current internal troubles

can be directly attributed, it seems, to the fact that four of her five ruling families have vanished over the course of the last several decades—some have fled the country in self-imposed and mysterious exile, while others were assassinated or hunted to extinction by mysterious enemies. The last surviving imperial family in Minkai, the Higashiyama, held onto the Jade Throne of Kasai until just 3 years ago, when Emperor Higashiyama Shigure was whisked away by his guards "for his own protection" to an undisclosed fortification. In the emperor's absence, rule of Minkai is the province of the empire's so-called Jade Regent. Unfortunately, as the years have worn on with no sign of that emperor's imminent return, this Jade Regent has grown ever more despotic and demanding. Many believe that the emperor is dead, and that the mysterious jade-armored figure known as the Jade Regent is in fact a pretender to the throne—yet the Higashiyama family continues to staunchly defend the man they put in the role of regent, thus keeping Minkai's eight provinces from outright rebellion. But while the province's leaders remain outwardly loyal, their citizens, emboldened by what seems a daily increase in unfair taxes, brutal police action, and ever more oppressive martial law, grow restless to the point of rebellion.

While Minkai awaits the final spark to trigger an all-out civil war, it does what it can to project a mien of strength and power. The government knows that if the empire were to look weak, its enemies would strike—already rumors of spies from Chu Ye, Wanshou, Bachuan, and even distant Lingshen and Shokuro circulate among political circles. The Jade Regent's increasing appetite for pleasure and power certainly makes continuing this facade more and more difficult, however.

**Kasai:** The capital of Minkai is also its largest city. Extensively planned, with numerous wide canals and meticulously designed districts, Kasai is one of the jewels of Minkai. Incoming trade and visitors are encouraged to make Kasai their first port of call by well-advertised promises of bargains and benefits for foreign visitors, so that Minkai's government can ensure that the first impression most visitors have of Minkai is this shining jewel of a city. The seat of the government and the site of the Imperial Palace, Kasai also features a deep harbor with abundant fishing.

**The Provinces:** Minkai is split into eight different provinces, each ruled by a separate governor responsible for the well-being of his or her people. Each province has its own responsibilities to the Jade Throne, be they supply of food, timber, artwork, military might, or whatever. Technically, a ninth province exists as well, consisting of the largely uncivilized northern and northeastern reaches of the immense peninsula. Here large tribes of barbarians, dangerous monsters, and ancient secrets rule.

## NAGAJOR

### Forbidding Serpentine Empire

**Alignment:** N

**Capital:** Zom Kullan (78,620)

**Notable Settlements:** Kaunendya (22,380), Thulsadus (39,820), Vannarak (25,970)

**Ruler:** First Mother Vassath Shethagri (LN female royal naga sorcerer 9)

**Government:** Ophidian matriarchy

**Major Races:** Nagaji, nagas

**Languages:** Nagaji, Tien

**Religion:** Desna, Lamashtu, Nalinivati, Tsukiyo, Yaezhing, Yamatsumi

**Resources:** Alchemical items, armor, clockworks, coal, coffee, gems, gold, iron, ivory, magic items, mercenaries, slaves, timber, weapons

Much of this large tropical realm is untamed and natural wilderness. Waterlogged jungles, lakes, swamps, and rivers make Nagajor a hot and humid land that suits the nature of its inhabitants—nagas and their reptilian vassals, the nagaji.

The current matriarchal naga dynasty has reigned over Nagajor for thousands of years. It is thought that the nagas originally came from Vudra long ago, but how they crossed the Embaral Ocean is unclear; most scholars suspect the nagas instead traveled through the Darklands. For their part, the nagas of Nagajor maintain that they have always been here—that the naga migration in fact went the other way, with nagas from Nagajor traveling west to Vudra many thousands of years ago.

Nagajor itself is one of the largest nations in Tian Xia, and while it is correct to observe that much of Nagajor remains wilderness, this statement marginalizes the extent of Nagajor's civilization. The empire itself is ruled by a First Mother—a role inherited for life—but the actual rule of Nagajor's numerous territories falls to individual naga matriarchs, all of whom are largely left to their own devices in determining how best to rule by the First Mother. The only overarching law is that no territory may harm a neighboring territory; this simple rule has kept Nagajor strong for ages, despite the fact that nagas of radically different personalities, desires, and ethics rule the territories. The number of territories varies, but generally hovers around two dozen—Nagajor has had 25 territories since the fall of Lung Wa, for example. A typical territory might include a small number of cities, a single large metropolis, dozens of tiny villages, or any combination thereof, with the borders of each territory generally being left to the wilds.

While some of Nagajor's nagas are benevolent, many are less so—and most of them prefer to deal with mammalian humanoids via their servitors, the nagaji. These reptilian humanoids were created in an ancient time by, it is said, Nalinvati herself, the first Queen of Nagajor and today the goddess of fertility and sorcery. While the nagaji were created as a laborer caste for the nagas, and while they continue to venerate the nagas who rule them almost as gods, the nagaji possess free will. They are not a mindless race of slaves—they continue to perform the bulk of Nagajor's work and leave matters of rule to their beloved matriarchs out of a fierce sense of national pride more than anything else.

**Zom Kullan:** A huge volcanically active mountain range called Kullan Dei winds its way through the center of Nagajor, with the capital, Zom Kullan, located inside a massive volcano that sits in the central core of the mountains. Rumors say that this volcano only remains dormant thanks to a complicated magical ritual that the naga royalty must constantly perform.

NAGAJOR TEMPLE

## PO LI

### Spiritual Stronghold of a Fallen Empire

**Alignment:** LN
**Capital:** Changdo (145,800)
**Notable Settlements:** Jitai
  (24,000), Tuotuo (19,150),
  Yuming (36,620)
**Ruler:** The Oracular Council
  (numerous high-level oracles)
**Government:** Theocracy
**Major Races:** Tian-Shus (also nagaji, samsarans, and
  Tian-Dtangs)
**Languages:** Tien
**Religion:** The Eternal Emperor (see below)
**Resources:** Artwork, cloth, fruit, holy relics, livestock,
  magic items, pork, seafood, timber

Although divine magic is seen as the greatest magic in Po Li, worship of the gods has long been forbidden in such close proximity to what was once Lung Wa's capital—the legendary Imperial City. Lung Wa's official religion was not a faith in the gods, but rather a faith in its leader, the so-called Eternal Emperor, master of the Oracular Council of Po Li. With the fall of Lung Wa, the worship of the gods has increased wildly in mainland Tian Xia, yet here in the lands known now as Po Li, oracular worship of the Eternal Emperor persists as a monotheistic religion that does not allow the participation of clerics—indeed, clerics are castigated as heretics. That the previous emperor perished during the fall of Lung Wa has not noticeably impacted the faith itself, for the people of Po Li know that it is but a matter of time before the Eternal Emperor is reincarnated and ascends once again to the *Five Dragon Throne*. Though the Oracular Council publicly supports the Emperor's claim to command of a unified Lung Wa, it has yet to produce a living heir. Skeptics suggest the theocrats are in no hurry to relinquish their tight control over the new nation of Po Li, while the faithful argue that the oracles await a sign from Heaven indicating that the true imperial heir has been reincarnated and is ready to unify the fractured empire.

Hopeful mothers often present their young children to the oracles with some claim of a divine sign that they have given birth to the emperor. Almost all such claims are dismissed by the investigating inquisitors, but a small fraction of such children are taken to be raised among the oracles. Many such children grow up to be members of the Oracular Council or else wandering heroes who defend the poor and defenseless citizens of Po Li.

The most famous exports of Po Li are holy relics. Blue-robed oracles—and blue-robed imposters claiming divine favor—sell bones, scraps of cloth, and ancient bits of jewelry to lords and peasants alike, claiming the items are genuine artifacts from the 66 virtuous emperors of fallen Lung Wa. Ninety-nine times out of a hundred, these items are worthless fakes, and those who sell them risk the wrath of the Oracular Council. But now and then, one of these holy relics carries within it strange and potent magic.

**Changdo, the Imperial City:** The original capital of Lung Wa, Changdo now serves as the seat of both temporal and spiritual power in Po Li. Here the bureaucracy consists primarily of oracles and their thousands of servants, who dispatch orders throughout the country. The innermost portion of Changdo is a city unto itself, off limits to all but the Oracular Council, their families, and their servants. Surrounding this forbidden zone are the manors and pavilions of secular lords and clerks. Beyond that is a bustling city of merchants, laborers, criminals, and beggars. The Imperial City has its own wonders as well—particularly the Eternal Emperor and the *Five Dragon Throne*.

**Emperor's Footprint:** This enormous sinkhole is a site of pilgrimage, rarely visited because of the many deadly monsters and hostile Sunsu Godae (see page 26) that dwell in the depths of the Chang Liao Jungle. Those oracles (and perhaps other casters of divine magic) who survive the journey to the Footprint discover a lush refuge surrounded by hanging vines and fresh waterfalls. Meditations in this serene location are said to connect pilgrims directly to the will of Heaven in the form of communion with one's patron deity. Legend also tells of a rare purple flower that blooms once every 144 years, the tales of its powers ranging from *geas* to *resurrection*, depending on the moral of the story.

**Eternal Emperor:** This colossal statue has been perpetually under construction for more than 300 years, each successive generation raising the elaborate structure another 10 stories or so above the height of the walls of Changdo. In recent decades, the people of Po Li have begun to believe that the Eternal Emperor will return incarnate only after the face of the statue is completed and his mortal form revealed. The more skeptical at court fear that the dangerous height of the statue suggests a plot to crush the imperial court at the crucial moment of the Emperor's eventual coronation.

**Five Dragon Throne:** A great seat of jade, ivory, chalcedony, lapis lazuli, and malachite sits empty at every meeting of the Oracular Council—this is the legendary *Five Dragon Throne*. Despite the legends that the artifact can control the weather and summon the great Sky Dragon, none dares sit upon the imperial throne. The last person to do so was instantly shriveled by a bolt from Heaven—although some historians hint that the bolt truly originated from a rival oracle on the council.

## QUAIN

### Land of a Thousand Heroes

**Alignment:** LN
**Capital:** Lanming (62,000)
**Notable Settlements:** Khitai (23,000), Nanzhu (34,000)
**Ruler:** King Wen (LN male Tian-Shu fighter 6/monk 9)
**Government:** Hereditary monarchy supported by a bureaucracy of eunuchs
**Major Races:** Tian-Shus (also kitsune and tengus)
**Languages:** Tien
**Religion:** Irori, Qi Zhong, Shizuru, Sun Wukong
**Resources:** Gems, gold, grain, mercenaries, paper, silk, stone, tea, timber

Without the military strength of Lingshen or the spiritual power of Po Li, Quain relies on the reputation of its many heroes for defense and glory. Thousands of practitioners of the martial arts are trained by its hundreds of different schools, clans, cults, temples, and houses. Many seek riches and glory. Others strive to prove the superiority of their school or even a specific style of personal combat. Some become dreadful villains, but more act as defenders of the people and—in times of war—of the nation. The exact number of martial arts masters operating in Quain at any one time varies wildly, but the total number is never less than several hundred—mystic balances are said to keep the total number of true masters at a static total of 1,000, with upsets and unexpected defeats of established masters interpreted as necessary "adjustments" as new masters rise in power.

Unlike the kings of some rival nations, the ruler of Quain hopes for many daughters rather than many sons, for only a royal maiden may exchange her heart for that of the legendary Celestial Dragon (a unique imperial dragon of incredible power) when it appears once each cycle of the zodiac (a 12-year period). The result is a *celestial pearl* that grants the power of a *wish*, traditionally used to ensure the country's prosperity for the next cycle. Last cycle, the self-proclaimed King of Heroes, now known as Burning Cloud Devil, disrupted the ceremony but failed to slay the Celestial Dragon. Only recently has Quain begun to recover from the resulting droughts and natural calamities.

Without an obvious source of power such as a large military or Po Li's divine strength, Quain has relied heavily on its large and educated bureaucracy of eunuchs. While tales of treachery among these childless men are popular, the truth is most are loyal and skilled servants of the kingdom. The best among them lead the country's armies, direct its commerce, gather its intelligence, and conduct the diplomacy that preserves Quain from the machinations of its neighbors.

The Golden River, one of the longest rivers in Tian Xia, serves as both the northern border for much of Quain and its primary trade route. Legend claims that its waters are the perspiration of the Celestial Dragon, which turns to gold at dawn and sunset.

**Dragon Temple:** This mountainside retreat dedicated to Irori is among the most respected and famous centers of martial arts training in all of Tian Xia. Aspirants from across the Dragon Empires, even as far as distant Minkai, make the long pilgrimage here to study.

**Eryiu Forest:** Nestled along the Wall of Heaven, the Eryiu Forest is a high-altitude woodland. While the infamous Temple of the Whispering Spider is perhaps the most well known of the strange ruins hidden within these woods, there are certainly many others waiting to be discovered by adventurers. The monkeys and apes of this woodland are particularly swift and unusually intelligent.

**House of 1,000 Silks:** While northern Quain is famous for its mulberry trees and the silkworms they feed, this silk-dyeing house is known throughout the Successor States for the magical qualities of its fabric. Many have tried to capture the house or steal the secret of its magics, but none have yet overcome the powerful martial arts of the sisters who own the establishment.

**Khitai:** Khitai never misses an opportunity for celebration or the trade that comes from foreign visitors eager to see its famous lion, dragon, and basilisk dancers.

**Lanming:** Home to the bureaucracy and all the major temples of the kingdom, the capital city bustles with activity, especially that caused by heroes testing their skills against rivals while demolishing local markets, tea houses, or brothels. Carpenters and masons throughout Quain have a saying: "To grow rich, move to Lanming."

**Nanzhu:** Notable for its vast and reportedly haunted cemetery on a hill above the city, Nanzhu is the center for most agricultural trade in the southeast. It is also home to many monkeys that wander freely during times of plenty and supplement the local diet in times of famine.

**Seething Hills:** Steam caverns and scalding geysers render this region uninhabitable to most humans, but agents from Nagajor favor the area for hideouts during their frequent infiltrations of their northern neighbor. Somewhere among the vast steam caverns beneath the hills, the great Four Winds Tortoise slumbers on a mound of golden treasure amassed over centuries.

**Temple of the Whispering Spider:** Once a temple devoted to Lao Shu Po, this ruin now serves as the lair of a giant arachnid said to be the cursed spirit of an ancient princess. Common folk of the area claim that only the Whispering Spider prevents monsters and evil spirits from flooding out of the ruins and preying upon the local people.

For more information on Quain, see the Pathfinder Tales novel *Master of Devils* by Dave Gross.

## SHAGUANG

### Desert of the Sky Spirits

**Alignment:** CN
**Capital:** None
**Notable Settlements:** Yjae (9,500)
**Ruler:** None
**Government:** Nomadic tribes living in awe and fear of mysterious sky spirits
**Major Races:** Tian-Las (also numerous desert and elemental races)
**Languages:** Auran, Hon-La
**Religion:** Desna, Lady Nanbyo, Lamashtu, Pharasma
**Resources:** Horses, livestock, mercenaries, slaves, stone

This vast desert was technically part of Lung Wa, but even at the empire's height no real attempt to map, colonize, or explore the desert was attempted. As such, the fall of Lung Wa had very little impact upon this region. Sprawling in the rain shadow of the highest reaches of the Wall of Heaven, a significant portion of this vast reach consists of sandy dunes, rocky badlands, barren salt flats, stony escarpments, and to the north, frozen swaths of tundra and cold desert. To the nomadic Tian-Las who dwell here, however, there is great beauty and wonder in the vistas that Shaguang has to offer. While the land is harsh, these tribes know of survival methods that make use of resources hidden in every shadow and under every stone. The tribes of Shaguang, known collectively as the Mutabi-qi, are quite numerous, but none truly know their total number.

The Mutabi-qi inhabit a network of oases connected by unmarked routes the nomads seasonally follow—these routes skirt vast, unexplored reaches of Shaguang, and grow fewer as one travels west toward the mountains. The desert's dangerous monsters include immense vermin, lean and pale bulettes, lamias, ash giants, death worms, and countless undead. These creatures grow more numerous the closer one gets to the Wall of Heaven, yet this is not the primary reason the Mutabi-qi see the desert's western reaches as taboo—for it is well known that the deep desert is the dominion of the Sky Spirits.

Each Mutabi-qi tribe has its own stories of the Sky Spirits. These tales are often contradictory and always fantastic—some speak of the black-skinned Sky Spirits being able to walk upon the air and of how they periodically take away children born with two different-colored eyes, while others warn that to look up during a storm is to invite a bolt of punishment. The one constant across all tales is that the Sky Spirits dwell in a magical flying city, and in this case, the legends are based entirely in fact.

**Yjae:** During the fall of the Shory civilization, the rulers of the city of Yjae enacted a controversial plan—when the end of the Shory seemed inevitable, the city of Yjae abandoned the nation and fled east across the Obari Ocean, soaring high above the clouds along the upper edges of the habitable skies. The city made the impossible journey only through the brilliance of its rulers and navigators, but when it reached the Wall of Heaven, it faced a nearly insurmountable barrier, for these mountain peaks stretched even higher than the Shory city could fly. Yjae's rulers attempted a treacherous navigation of the lowest passes they could find, yet powerful winds and other, stranger influences that seemed to rise from the eerie ruins on the stark mountain slopes seized the flying city and tossed it like a leaf in a typhoon. The city smashed against a mountainside, crushing nearly a quarter of its towers and understructure and nearly sending it spiraling into the ground. Worse, strange denizens of the high mountains invaded the city when it slipped through a thin place between reality and the nightmare realm of Leng.

With a quarter of the city in ruins, its magical method of propulsion irrevocably destroyed, and sinister denizens of a nightmare dimension seizing control of certain parts of the city's understructure and damaged towers, Yjae's navigators managed, somehow, to maintain control and slide down the far side of the Wall's thermals. But the damage was done—while Yjae still floats, its ability to move on its own has been lost. Since that fateful crossing, Yjae has drifted with the winds, stuck forever in the eddies and rivers of air that churn miles above the deep desert below. Using magical flight, the people of Yjae make regular trips to the ground below in order to gather supplies, but they keep contact with the Mutabi-qi to a minimum. Although the stories the Mutabi-qi tell of the Shory are often sinister, the Shory themselves are not evil—they simply wish to limit knowledge of their city as long as its ability to defend itself remains compromised.

Today, the people of Yjae have forgotten much of the magic they once knew, but they continue to toil in their laboratories and libraries as best they can, hoping someday to learn the secrets of their legacy again so they can repair the damage done to their city and continue their journey east. The ruined quarters of the city are still rife with strange monsters and unpredictable magic from their ancient brush against Leng, yet these monsters have been contained by several powerful wards. The need for maintenance of these wards further slows the Shory's progress in repairing their city, to say nothing of the fact that the invaders still control the portion of the city wherein Yjae's propulsion system was housed. Still, the people of Yjae know that they are the last surviving carriers of the Shory legacy—the protection of that legacy is their greatest charge.

## SHENMEN

### Cursed Land of Spiders and Ghosts

**Alignment:** NE
**Capital:** Yin-Sichasi (4,900)
**Notable Settlements:** Baakai
(3,300), Pek Peh (2,610),
Sze (1,600)
**Ruler:** Lady Lang Loi (NE female jorogumo witch 14)
**Government:** Loose alliance of bandit lords ruled by
monsters
**Major Races:** Tian-shus (also evil fey, jorogumos,
wayangs, and other monsters)
**Languages:** Aklo, Tien
**Religion:** Fumeiyoshi, Lady Nanbyo, Lao Shu Po, Pharasma
**Resources:** Darkwood, silver, timber

During Lung Wa's rule, Shenmen was something of a backwater province. Relatively close to the empire's core, Shenmen's gloomy weather patterns only rarely allowed for honestly sunny days. Moss grew everywhere that fungus did not, and the only break between the frequent storms was the endless drizzle. Yet the lumber of Spectrewood and the ample veins of silver in the eastern Gossamers ensured that Lung Wa would never simply let this province be forgotten. The citizens of Shenmen were expected to produce silver and timber at a constant rate to supply the empire's need—and the fact that Lung Wa generally saved government and overseer posts in Shenmen as a sort of punishment for nobles and officials who had shamed themselves or broken the law only further added to the land's miseries. Yet as long as the silver and timber continued to flow from Shenmen's borders, Lung Wa kept the roads and villages relatively safe.

That ended with Lung Wa's fall. Cut off from their resources and unable to swiftly flee, the government officials stationed in Shenmen's villages and the overseers in charge of its mines and logging camps swiftly reverted to the corruption and criminal activities that landed them posts in Shenmen in the first place, and Shenmen's citizens suffered. But when the monsters rose, these leaders were the first to fall, and their horrific deaths resulted in their spirits rising as ghosts or worse more often than not.

The monsters that plague Shenmen run a wide gamut, from relatively mindless vermin to more sinister creatures like ettercaps, evil fey, and murderous wayangs. Undead, particularly ghosts and other incorporeal threats, are frighteningly common but tend not to drift too far from favored haunts. But above all, the greatest nightmare of Shenmen are the jorogumos of the Gossamer Mountains. Legend holds that when a spider grows old enough, it undergoes a blasphemous metamorphosis into the form of a beautiful human woman—whether or not this tale is true, the seductive jorogumos pull the political strings of Shenmen. In turn, the jorogumos are ruled by their own cruel witch-queen, the Lady Lang Loi, who dwells in Yin-Sichasi, a hauntingly beautiful underground city under the Gossamer Mountains said to house thousands of the witch-queen's favored slaves.

The leaders of Shenmen's towns and villages are generally kept in thrall to a jorogumo, either via magic or fear, and the selection of several young men each year as sacrifices to the jorogumo falls to those leaders. In order to prevent their people from rising up against them, most of these leaders have turned to the despicable practice of abducting travelers and victims from neighboring lands— in this way, the nightmares of Shenmen have turned its people into bandits or worse.

JOROGUMO

## SHOKURO

### Kingdom of Exiled Samurai

**Alignment:** LN
**Capital:** Mukinami (22,870)
**Notable Settlements:** Fortress Taufoon (2,930), Gau Bie (4,840), Khaeshek (2,000), Tupai (17,476)
**Ruler:** Shokuro Toriaka, the Sun Shogun (LN male Tian-Min samurai 14)
**Government:** Shogunate
**Major Races:** Tian-Mins, Tian-Shus (also elves, kitsune, and Taldans)
**Languages:** Elven, Minkaian, Tien
**Religion:** Abadar, Daikitsu, General Susumu, Pharasma, Shizuru
**Resources:** Fruit, grain, livestock, mercenaries, tea, vegetables

This fertile land once served as one of Lung Wa's breadbaskets. Four closely allied provinces, each specializing in a different crop, toiled night and day to provide much of Lung Wa with the fruits, vegetables, grain, and tea the empire demanded. When Lung Wa fell, the leader of each realm became convinced that he and he alone should rule the four provinces, and the resulting conflict was swift and brutal. No one emerged the winner, and the croplands burned.

Several years later, Lingshen annexed the land. Eager to rebuild the region as a provider of foodstuffs, Lingshen pressed the lands' surviving peasants into backbreaking servitude, forcing them at spearpoint to rebuild. Time and time again, the people attempted to rebel against Lingshen, but time and time again Lingshen's superior forces crushed and punished these rebellions. As the land grew closer to productivity and rebellions came less often, Lingshen turned its attentions elsewhere—to Kaoling, to Quain, and to Po Li. Its leaders felt confident that they had these provinces under control, and that confidence is what lost them one of their greatest resources.

In 7176 IC, a charismatic samurai named Toriaka was exiled from Minkai for daring to slay a corrupt lord. Minkai's government secretly approved of Toriaka's actions, but could not let his insolence go unpunished, and so sent him into exile—by far the least cruel of the punishments that tradition demanded. Toriaka accepted the judgment stoically, and many of his loyal followers chose to become ronin as well in order to accompany him into his exile. Eager to see the world, Toriaka looked to the old stories of a heroic samurai named Shokuro for inspiration. In those tales, Shokuro supposedly encountered a strange race of "beautiful, sharp-eared people who dwelled in a tree of silver." These tales captivated Toriaka's heart, and he set out to travel through the war-torn Dragon Empires to meet these people. His travels brought him across Xidao and through poverty-stricken Kwanlai and the recently conquered lands of Amanandar, and finally he reached Jinin and its storied citizens.

Yet Toriaka's delight at meeting the elves of Shokuro's tales was blunted by witnessing the cruelties unfolding to the south. In the farmlands now ruled by Lingshen, Toriaka saw the same arrogance and cruelty of the lord he slew back in Minkai, only taken to a horrific extreme. Here, Toriaka saw his new cause. With support from Jinin and Amanandar, he led his ronin into the farmlands and began to organize the beleaguered people into a proper resistance. Now led by a brilliant tactician rather than desperate peasants, the people of the land rallied, and before Lingshen realized what had happened, Toriaka had accomplished a deed worthy of a new legend—he had liberated a nation.

Since his surprising capture of the land, the Sun Shogun has transformed the region into a potent military machine. Threats of destruction to the recently reclaimed land combined with brilliant tactics and solid defenses have, to date, kept any significant reprisals from Lingshen from bringing further harm to the land. And with each year that Shokuro continues to offer Lingshen fair and affordable prices for the tea and food produced in these lands, Lingshen's need for revenge against the land lessens.

**Mukinami:** Once a free city where the four provinces could meet to engage in free trade, Mukinami is now the capital of Shokuro and the seat of the Sun Shogun's palace. In order to ensure the cooperation of the people, the Sun Shogun allowed the heirs of the four families of the original provinces positions of power as an advisory council known collectively as the Four Pillars, yet these four families are finding it difficult to set aside their traditional bickering and grudges.

**Sea of Eels:** To the west, Shokuro is bordered by The Sea of Eels, a wide but relatively shallow body of water. The eastern shores of the sea serve Shokuro as its primary trade route, and numerous small fishing villages dot the coastline. Each of these villages is well protected by a small garrison and a growing navy. The fisherfolk of these villages have long been beset by enormous predatory eels with strange magical powers. Attacks from these eels were traditionally fended off by an old defensive pact between the coastal villages and a group of aquatic kami known as the Makaitsu. But recently, the Makaitsu seem to have disappeared without warning and the strange eels have returned. Local officials have posted bounties for eel carcasses, and the fishing magnates have petitioned the capital of Mukinami to help them solve the mysterious disappearance of their kami allies.

## TIANJING

**Beloved of the Heavens**

**Alignment:** NG
**Capital:** Zetang (26,370)
**Notable Settlements:** Desyo (9,380), Kerisen (11,090), Sutakei (14,920)
**Ruler:** Onishi Kazujun, First Speaker for the Council (NG male aasimar cleric of Shelyn 15)
**Government:** Custodian council of elderly advisors
**Major Races:** Aasimars (also samsarans, tengus, Tian-Mins, Tian-Shus, and Tian-Sings)
**Languages:** Celestial, Tien
**Religion:** Desna, Kofusachi, Qi Zhong, Shelyn, Tsukiyo, empyreal lords
**Resources:** Artwork, cloth, clothing, dyes, gold, horses, livestock, paper, spices, sugar, timber, wool

In the long-forgotten past, a host of holy beings from the good-aligned planes fought in a great war against a tide of ancient evil: a qlippoth horde that threatened to infest the Material Plane. The celestial host swung the tide of the long war and secured victory, but at great cost—they suffered enormous losses in the war and were not able to properly repair the rifts between the deepest reaches of the Abyss and the Material Plane. In order to guard forevermore against a recrudescence of the qlippoth uprising in this idyllic land, the archons, azatas, agathions, and angels who had fought side by side accepted exile to the Material Plane. They settled in this land, and as humans rose in power, the celestials welcomed the best of them into their guarded lands. In time, the celestials saw that their descendants had grown numerous enough to take over defense of the land from them, and they finally returned home to the Outer Planes, leaving the land of Tianjing in the capable hands of their aasimar children.

As human empires rose and fell, the land of Tianjing always treated with them fairly and greeted them with open arms. Those who accepted these offerings of peace were allowed to wander among Tianjing's many temples and utopian landscapes, but those who sought instead to conquer and control Tianjing found the aasimar nation, as peaceful as it seemed, incredibly difficult to take. For the aasimars were charged with protecting the realm from ancient horrors from before the time of the gods themselves—what worry was it to guard their borders against mere mortals?

Tianjing was one of the few existing nations that Lung Wa, in a surprising show of restraint and wisdom, allowed to exist without attempting to overtake, for the emperor at the time rightfully concluded that to undertake war against

a backdrop of such beauty and wonder would surely damn him and his people to Hell. Indeed, he adopted almost the reverse of the philosophy Lung Wa had for other lands—rather than invade and conquer, he sent support to Tianjing in the form of food, art, and anything else he felt the aasimars might desire.

Tianjing was ill prepared when Lung Wa crumbled. The many centuries of support from Lung Wa had allowed Tianjing to abandon self-support in favor of the pursuit of art and philosophy, and it now found itself alone and without a steady source of food and protection, bordered by aggressive Successor States and indifferent neighbors with problems of their own. Tianjing increasingly found itself assaulted by small but eager bands of bandits, exiled armies, and worse, and for the first time since the ancient wars with the qlippoth, its cities and wilds were stained with the blood of warfare.

From such anarchy, however, came eventual salvation—if only at the last moment, as the aasimars teetered on the edge of oblivion. This salvation came in the form of a compelling and enigmatic young aasimar woman by the name of Sulunai. Hers was the calm voice of reason during a time of chaos. She single-handedly brought about Tianjing's salvation, and today, the nation is well on the way to recovering from the atrocities it suffered after the fall of Lung Wa.

Yet this recovery has had an unforeseen ripple, for in focusing on defending themselves from banditry and invading armies, and then in recovering their self-sufficiency and restoring their temple cities, the people of Tianjing have neglected their duties to guard the ancient portals to the deep Abyss. So long had the threat of the qlippoth been quelled that the ancient warnings were all but forgotten, and today, while outwardly presenting a facade of beauty and light, Tianjing fights an increasingly desperate battle within itself.

**Kaimuko Wood:** This extensive woodland harbors many aasimar villages—it was to these woods that the aasimars retreated during the darkest times after the fall of Lung Wa. Today, ironically, the deepest parts of this woodland hide the worst of the Abyssal rents through which the qlippoth are regaining a foothold in the world, and the borders of these hideous blighted portions of woodland are barely patrolled by desperate aasimars who fear that they are but months, perhaps days, away from a disastrous otherworldly invasion.

**Zetang:** Situated on the beautiful Point Aykishe on Tianjing's east coast, the glittering city of Zetang has been completely restored to its former beauty after being sacked by an eager navy of Zo pirates not long after Lung Wa's fall. The city's three harbors are strewn with sunken pirate ships to this day, and the waters are reputedly haunted by the angry ghosts of the dead, yet even if these tales are true, this unnatural stain does nothing to diminish Zetang's glory.

## VALASHMAI JUNGLE

### Here There Be Monsters

**Alignment:** CN
**Capital:** None
**Notable Settlements:** None
**Ruler:** None
**Government:** None
**Major Races:** Catfolk, grippli, lizardfolk, xills, various degenerate humanoids, monsters
**Languages:** Abyssal, Catfolk, Draconic, Grippli, Infernal, pidgin Tien
**Religion:** Lamashtu, numerous demigods and forgotten cults
**Resources:** Ancient magic and hidden secrets (see below)

Across this vast untamed landscape spreads a seemingly endless expanse of luxuriant jungle foliage. While the Valashmai Jungle is a place of terror that treats all who venture within as intruders to be consumed, some brave explorers have found evidence that even here, in one of the most dangerous reaches of the Dragon Empires, civilization was not always an alien concept. Strange ruins and lost cities are scattered throughout the jungle and mountains of the region—proportioned not for humans but a race nearly three times their size. Very little is known of this mysterious race of reptilian giants, aside from a few fragments that reveal them as the Valashaians—from which the name of the region as it is known today was derived. Certainly, as more expeditions to the ruins of Valashai are successfully undertaken, more information about the mysterious Valashaians will come to light, but for now their secrets remain lost in the jungle's embrace.

Solitary creatures of great power, such as dragons, exiled outsiders, enormous monsters known as kaiju, mu spores, and strange undead horrors are known to dwell in various parts of the Valashmai Jungle alongside more mundane but no less dangerous creatures like dinosaurs, carnivorous plants, exotic wild animals, and hideously oversized vermin. Lesser races, such as catfolk, grippli, and lizardfolk, are quite numerous in the jungle—their tribes vary in size and outlook, although savagery is generally the rule in such wild environs. Perhaps the most feared of Valashmai's denizens are the xills—while xills are normally natives of the Ethereal Plane, the xills of Valashmai are green-scaled native outsiders who dwell in the ruins of Valashai and conduct frequent raids against neighboring tribes of humanoids, taking slaves to serve as incubators for their ravenous young. Among these unusually chaotic xills, arcane magic is greatly respected and prized, and each xill tribe is led by a powerful sorcerer or summoner with ties to the Abyss.

**Chenlun Mountains:** Of the Valashmai Jungle's two significant mountain ranges, the jagged peaks known as the Chenlun Mountains are the larger and more volcanic. Here, tribes of fire giants led, in many cases, by powerful fire yai hold dominion over the surrounding lands.

**Goroyasa:** Off the southwestern shore of Valashmai looms the great island of Goroyasa, a realm whose plant and animal life share a single hideous affliction—a foul fungal growth of various shades that infests anything organic and grants strange powers while simultaneously robbing the life forms of their free will. The slaves of Goroyasa, as the degenerate human tribes that dwell on the isle are called, venerate the demon lord Cyth-V'sug, but whether that foul entity has plans for (or even knows about) the region is unknown.

**Kashang:** In the eastern foothills of the Chenlun Mountains lies a many-tiered succession of stepped temple edifices, deeply shrouded by the ever-present jungle. The jungle around these Valashaian ruins is deathly quiet—not even fiercest prowling jungle creature disturbs the clammy, unnatural silence of the slick, dark stones of Kashang. The horrors contained within have swelled and grown strong during the long centuries since their summoning by the forgotten race that built the place. They endlessly wait for intruders to disturb and inadvertently rupture the delicate bonds of the dark rituals that constrain them. The forbidden lore within Kashang is old and powerful, but there is a steep price to pay for it.

**Star Titan's Grave:** Stories speak of a megalithic construction the size of a city but with the shape of a vast humanoid who fell from the sky in ancient times, plummeting into Valashmai's tangled emerald heart. Many historical figures claim to have witnessed the ill-omened falling star shoot across the night sky of Tian Xia, but beyond narrowing where it fell to somewhere in eastern Valashmai, Xa Hoian astrologers were unable to chart its exact landing site. Since the object's fall, no less than two dozen explorers have claimed to have found the Star Titan's Grave. The most reputable of these, however, perished soon thereafter from a hideous affliction that melted skin from bone and resisted all attempts at magical cures—the secrets of what they learned at the Star Titan's Grave went with them to their own.

**Sudisan Peaks:** Valashmai's smaller mountain range may lack the Chenlun Mountains' volcanic legacy, but the mountains themselves are, if anything, even more inhospitable. Plants here grow unnaturally well—most are toxic or poisonous, some have acidic sap, and many have evolved into dangerous killing organisms. A wide variety of leafy subspecies of the assassin vine grow throughout the peaks, and snapperjaw giant flytraps are numerous. Groves of fungus-covered tendriculoses thrive in the valleys lodged between the peaks, growing alongside massive viper vines and even stranger verdant horrors.

## WALL OF HEAVEN

### Where Earth Meets Sky

**Alignment:** N
**Capital:** None
**Notable Settlements:**
Dap-Cha
Monastery (2,400),
Zhu-Cho (3,100)
**Ruler:** None
**Government:** None
**Major Races:** Tian-Las, Tian-Shus (also giants, oni, yetis, and worse)
**Languages:** Aklo, Hon-La, Senzar, Tien
**Religion:** Desna, Irori, Lamashtu, Tsukiyo, Yamatsumi
**Resources:** Copper, gems, gold, iron, livestock (primarily yaks), silver, stone

The indomitable mountains known as the Wall of Heaven tower almost beyond mortal comprehension. This chain of peaks stretches from the arctic circle almost to the equator, and as such is the longest mountain range on Golarion. The jagged teeth of this vast range encompass countless mountaintops, many of which are in excess of 30,000 feet in height. The mountains have sacred names—Lamjung ("Dawn Herald"), Kanchung-La ("Peak That Has No Footprints"), and Targ Kang ("Tower to Heaven"). The mightiest peaks lie west of Shaguang, in a region known as Gorak Tcho, a realm rumored to share many links to the nightmare realm of Leng. The greatest mountain, the Himcho ("Mother of the World"), towers at a staggering height of 37,400 feet. Pilgrims of various gods make their way to temples at its mighty feet; only those with magical protection can survive the eternal winter amid the airless peaks of these mountains.

The weather among these mountains is the stuff of a thousand thousand tales. Storms of incredible fury appear in minutes from nowhere, avalanches that could bury cities fall as the spring thaws hit, and monsoons drown valleys and cause colossal mud waves to tear down valleys. Winters are worse, and little moves in the mountains during these times save yetis and other monstrous denizens. Life only thrives in the lower pastures, which are augmented by summer grazing meadows high above.

Incredibly remote passes cross a few valleys, but these are both tortuous and dangerous. Only the most foolhardy risk these routes to cross the mountains, and even then, very little waits to reward them for their toil on the slopes facing the Embaral Ocean. Only where the Wall of Heaven breaks into a (still quite high-altitude) pass is travel relatively safe—but the city of Goka rules this region.

Monks, oracles, and other hermits make their homes in all parts of the mountains. Some orders (such as those of Irori) prefer seclusion, and build incredible monasteries on high slopes and passes. The Iroran Doan Monastery, which perches atop the Lamjung Pass, is one of the most spectacular, hanging above the infamous Wall of Lamjung, a 6,000-foot-high sheer cliff overlooking the Gokan Saddle. The largest monastery is the waterfall-enveloped Dap-Cha Monastery near the headwaters of the Miochi River—this monastery is the size of a large town.

The upper valleys are home to large numbers of yetis as well, and these towering creatures are the unofficial "keepers" of the Wall of Heaven. It is said that none know the secrets and perils of the Wall better than yetis, and while these creatures are often quick to attack those who brazenly intrude, they rarely trouble the high mountain villages of humans who choose to dwell there.

**Iron Mountain:** The overland route to Iron Mountain passes through this region of towering peaks whose overgrown tops appear as islands floating among the clouds. Called the Flying Mountains, this region is home to enormous beasts and strange flora that live among the perpetual shadows of the deep canyons. High among the peaks of Iron Mountain, an ancient platform surrounded by sentinel statues of foo lions and other creatures marks the site of twin gates, one leading to Heaven, the other to Hell. Once every 12 years, a powerful imperial dragon known to the people of Quain as the Celestial Dragon appears to grant a wish to a royal maiden.

**Koeh Lau:** Stories persist of Koeh Lau—a place hidden somewhere in an incredibly remote valley in the northern stretches of the Wall. The valley is said to be like heaven on earth, a land of plenty where all human evils are unknown and the valley's enlightened residents need no ruler. The reality is different. In truth, Koeh Lau is a forbidden city populated by vampiric monks, oracles, and witches who use the idyllic city as a place to keep their human "pets" content during the day so they can feed and cavort among them at night to their black hearts' content.

**Menhu Leng:** Stories of the horrors of Leng, said to be accessible by the lost, dreaming minds of slumbering mortals, are well known throughout Tian Xia. That Leng lies very near to the central portion of the Wall of Heaven is known as well—philosophers theorize that the Wall's peaks are so high and so sharp that they rasped thin the barriers between reality and nightmare. Others simply believe that denizens from Leng worked in primeval times to ensure a perpetual link between their realm and this one at that location. Whatever the cause, the ominous basalt ruins of the cursed city of Menhu Leng are ruled by that land's denizens, monstrous creatures who ride the backs of shantak birds when they need to descend to the Dragon Empires on sinister missions.

## WANSHOU

### Post-Apocalyptic Kraken-Ruled Swampland

**Alignment:** CE
**Capital:** Numijaan (17,890)
**Notable Settlements:** Aoriika
(7,740), Minnsiat (11,302), Payothu (8,620)
**Ruler:** Zhanagorr (CE male elder kraken)
**Government:** Monstrous tyranny
**Major Races:** Boggards, kappas, Tian-Mins, Tian Shus
**Languages:** Aquan, Boggard, Minkaian, Tien
**Religion:** Hei Feng, Lady Nanbyo, Lamashtu, Lao Shu Po
**Resources:** Grain (primarily rice), mercenaries, ship
supplies, ships, slaves

As part of Imperial Lung Wa, Wanshou diligently served its purpose as a center of food production. This nation once boasted vast, extensively irrigated reaches dedicated to the production of rice, which was then exported throughout the Dragon Empires. When Lung Wa collapsed, Wanshou suffered perhaps more than any other region in the Dragon Empires—certainly its fall from one of the empire's most valued holdings to its current hellish state is the stuff of legend.

As Lung Wa began to fall apart, things quickly turned sour in Wanshou. Its citizens, already worked to the breaking point by the empire, rose up in revolt against the remaining imperial troops. Cities shook and fields burned as the nation tore itself apart from within. The rebels had little time to enjoy their successful uprising, though, for a number of torrential storms soon struck the nation. Even though Wanshou was no longer wracked by revolution, weathering the floods and winds of such storms was a harrowing ordeal—in the absence of any organized preparation, the nation was devastated. And when things looked their darkest, a cabal of desperate oracles called out to primal powers for deliverance from the doom they had in part brought upon themselves.

What answered this anguished call was not fate, salvation, or the gods. What answered was the monstrous entity Zhanagorr.

Whether Zhanagorr heard the oracles' call or simply happened to come upon Wanshou after being dredged from the depths of Xidao by the self-same typhoon that was flooding the nation quickly became irrelevant. An elder kraken with midnight-black flesh, Zhanagorr entered the coastal capital of Numijaan accompanied by tsunamis and storms of lightning so furious that the city itself was all but destroyed. Nearly 80 percent of the sprawling metropolis was swept out to sea—those few who

survived did so purely by chance. But just as Wanshou's chances seemed to be at an end, the kraken proved to be the nation's sinister salvation. The kraken called upon its magic to end the typhoon and saved Wanshou from obliteration. Zhanagorr's price, as the sodden survivors would quickly learn, was Wanshou itself.

Today, many believe that the strangely potent typhoon that set up Wanshou's domination by its kraken overlord was in fact engineered and manipulated by Zhanagorr. The kraken's methods of keeping its enslaved nation in line and under control are not limited to the manipulation of the weather and the water, however. In the century since Zhanagorr's conquest of Wanshou, much of the nation has reverted to swampland, the once-fertile rice paddies swiftly returning to wilderness. With the kraken's rise in power has come an equal rise among the monstrous races of the swamp. Boggards and kappas in particular have grown more and more common; these creatures are the favored minions of the kraken and serve as Wanshou's nobility, military, and priesthood alike. The descendants of those humans unfortunate enough to survive Wanshou's near destruction now toil as slaves of the state.

Perhaps the most horrible facet of Wanshou, though, is the fact that not all of the land's humans serve as slaves. A growing number of men and women regard Zhanagorr as a benevolent god-king, and see him as their savior. Some of this veneration is born from ignorance, but insanity and self-hatred are increasingly common causes of this behavior. What Zhanagorr's actual goals in Wanshou are remains a mystery, but the kraken certainly seems eager to stockpile wealth and resources. The most common theory to explain the kraken's motivations is that it is preparing to launch a war against Xidao—certainly, the locathahs of Xidao treat Wanshou as a very serious threat indeed.

**Chotilema's Boudoir:** Deep in the western foothills leading up to mountains of Zi Ha lies the Sunken Valley of Chotilema, a flooded gorge fed by both mountain streams and overflow from the lowland marshes. Swamp hags, oozes, and innumerable leeches inhabit the area. Villagers say that the place is the cursed burial ground of the powerful bog witch Chotilema. Weed-choked underwater tunnels lead to a chain of fetid caverns clogged with molds and slime where Chotilema once worked her putrid magics. Here lurk her obscene creations: a seeping throng of septic undead abominations that have never seen the light of day.

**Numijaan:** Once one of Lung Wa's largest cities, the ruined skeleton of Numijaan is now populated by a tenth of the numbers it once housed—and most of its "citizens" are boggards or kappas. Large swaths of Numijaan are underwater, either sunken or scooped away by the tsunamis and floodwaters of a century ago—here and there, the tops of stone buildings still protrude from the mud.

## XA HOI

### Empire of the Dragon

**Alignment:** LN

**Capital:** Ngon Hoa (148,400)

**Notable Settlements:** An Son (41,345), Da Miem (39,950), Hon Rach (22,240), My Thien (98,800)

**Ruler:** His Supreme Draconic Majesty, Dragon King Pham Duc Quan (N great wyrm sovereign dragon)

**Government:** Draconic monarchy

**Major Races:** Tian-Dans (also nagaji, Tian-Dtangs, Tian-Hwans, and wayangs)

**Languages:** Draconic, Tien

**Religion:** Abadar, General Susumu, Irori, Nalinivati, Shizuru

**Resources:** Dyes, iron, gold, livestock, pearls, ship supplies, ships, spices, timber

How a nation of humans came to be ruled by sovereign imperial dragons in human guise is one of the greatest mysteries in Tian Xia's history. Pham Duc Quan is the thirteenth monarch of Xa Hoi and can trace his pedigree in an unbroken line to the first Dragon King, Pham Toan Rong, nearly 3 millennia ago. His brothers and sisters serve as the generals of his extensive humanoid army, known as the Dragon's Teeth. Quan ascended the throne many decades before Lung Wa's collapse, and the stability he offered Xa Hoi during the time of chaos helped the nation emerge as one of the greatest powers in the Dragon Empires after the dust of Lung Wa's fall cleared. Today, Xa Hoi enjoys positive relations with most of its civilized neighbors and stands ever vigilant against threats from the Valashmai wilderness. Quan has also ordered a significant expansion of Xa Hoi's navy, which now patrols the kingdom's coast and acts as a check on Minatan piracy.

The humanoid population of Xa Hoi is organized into thousands of clans, with more meaning given to regional affinity than race; humans and other races like nagaji or wayangs often intermingle in the same clans, though such intermixed clans tend to live in the northwestern mining region of the Kim Loai Hills. Worship of several deities is common in Xa Hoi, and the people also erect shrinelike monuments to their draconic leader and the 12 sovereign dragons who ruled before him as well. These shrines are more objects of adoration than they are places of proper worship, but the subtle distinction in how Tian-Dans honor these different types of shrines certainly gives rise to the misconception that the people of Xa Hoi worship their emperors as gods. Splendid pagodas to the Dragon Spirit of Precision, the Multifold Dragon Heart, the Dragon's Penetrating Eye, and others are scattered across Xa Hoi, with a vast network of monks and historians assiduously attending each. The industrious nation is celebrated for the exemplary shipyards of Hon Rach, the exquisite pearls found along the coast of the Con Rong Da Peninsula, and the profitable fisheries along its major rivers.

Justice is harsh in Xa Hoi. Aside from exorbitant fines for minor transgressions, three punishments are the norm: death, disfigurement, and conscription. A cutpurse may lose a thumb, a gang of crucified highway brigands might line the road they once plagued, a merchant who cheats a government agent may find himself serving for the rest of his life as captain's scribe aboard a Minata-bound warship. Courts are presided over by dragon-masked judges reputed for their incorruptibility.

**Ngon Hoa:** One of Tian Xia's largest cities, the capital of Ngon Hoa rises majestically from Xa Hoi's heart at the convergence of the Shung and the Ban Chuy Rivers. It seems that every building in this city is a towering monument to architecture, and the hundreds of masterfully crafted hanging bridges that connect the towers and the winding canals that separate them allow citizens to live their entire lives without ever setting foot on the ground if such is their desire.

### DRAGON KING PHAM DUC QUAN

## XIDAO

### War-Weary Aquatic Nation

**Alignment:** N

**Capital:** Yashabaru (22,400)

**Notable Settlements:** Mewru (7,200), Pobashabla (12,450), Uruuknus (11,210)

**Ruler:** High Matriarch Urakadussi (N female locathah oracle 14)

**Government:** Matriarchy of loosely affiliated city states

**Major Races:** Locathahs (also cecaelias, krakens, merrows, sahuagin, and tritons)

**Languages:** Aquan, Tien

**Religion:** Hei Feng, Nalinivati, Qi Zhong, various demigods

**Resources:** Artwork, coral, jewelry, pearls, seafood, sunken treasures

This shallow sea known as the Xidao Gulf separates Minkai from mainland Tian Xia. It is frequented by superstitious fishermen and merchants, ever careful to pay homage to the creatures beneath. The shallow shores of the sea are home to many shellfish; crabs, lobsters and other shellfish abound here and act as a draw to fishermen. Xidao's pearls are famed throughout Minkai for their beauty, and black pearls of great value are often found here. Those who would travel upon or take resources from the Xidao Gulf are well advised to pay for the honor, however, by placing an offering in one of the countless "trade spires" scattered atop reefs and atolls throughout the gulf. These stone obelisks feature numerous small shelves onto which offerings of ceramics, glass, gold, metal tools and weapons, and vegetables like tubers can be placed. Travelers or fishermen who fail to place these offerings do so at significant risk, for the gulf is far more than a mere waterway—it is an aquatic nation.

The primary denizens of Xidao are the fishlike humanoids known as locathahs. Other creatures, such as the octopoid cecaelias and the benevolent tritons, dwell in Xidao as well, but the locathahs are the rulers of this nation. They monitor the trade spires and the offerings placed there, and in return they help protect air breathers who wish to use Xidao for travel or fishing. They generally take no aggressive action against sailors and fishermen who fail to place offerings, but neither do they come to the aid of those people when the more sinister denizens of Xidao inevitably take advantage of the lack of locathah protection.

Xidao itself consists of numerous undersea city-states; each has its own government and leaders, but all operate under a treaty that ensures not only that no city-state shall take hostile acts against another, but also that if one city-state comes under attack, the others will come to its defense. Local politics and outlooks are varied, and while a few of Xidao's city-states have little interest in "air gulpers" (a term of disdain the locathahs use for non-aquatic races), most are willing to trade with sailors and fishermen on neighboring coastlines.

**Aya-Maru:** Despite the relatively peaceful philosophies of Xidao, the nation itself has not known true peace for thousands of years. Splitting Xidao down the middle is a great underwater trench known as Aya-Maru. While the depth of the Xidao Gulf is rarely more than a few hundred feet, the Aya-Maru trench plunges well over 3 miles straight down into an inky black abyss of perpetual darkness. Many locathahs believe that Aya-Maru is bottomless—that it leads directly into some deep underwater Hell. It is from the depths of Aya-Maru that Xidao's enemies have long waged war on the locathahs. The sheer walls of the trench are riddled with caverns that serve as the lairs of a staggering number of bickering merrows and sahuagin—were these countless tribes ever to unify under a single leader, they would swarm out of Aya-Maru to slaughter the inhabitants of Xidao. As it stands, the constant tiny raids on the submerged realms that border Aya-Maru keep Xidao from ever truly feeling at peace. Yet the merrows and sahuagin are not what Xidao fears the most about Aya-Maru, for at its deepest reaches, krakens rule. Fortunately, the krakens of Aya-Maru only rarely come to the surface—and those that do are invariably outcasts from the depths.

**Wai-Gaa:** Also known as "insubstantial lands," wai-gaa occasionally rise from the depths as portions of the deep mud and ooze on the sea floor break away and, borne by trapped gasses, float to the surface. Sometimes these floating islands are littered with curious ancient temples or are inhabited by the undead victims of sunken ships, while at other times strange beasts flop and churn in shallow ponds of life-giving water. These places are perilous not only for inhabitants thrust suddenly into the air, but also for air-breathing visitors, as they inevitably descend into the seas once more, and with shocking speed—many overly curious scholars have been dragged to a watery grave when the gases giving a wai-gaa support finally give out.

**Yashabaru:** The largest of the locathah city-states, Yashabaru is a breathtaking city of brilliantly colored coral towers and seashell-encrusted domes. Traditionally the home of Xidao's greatest matriarchs, the city is currently ruled by a powerful oracle named Urakadussi—while she does not technically have the power to command other cities in Xidao, most of the locathahs view her as their leader and would lay down their lives for her honor if asked.

## ZI HA

### Sacred Land of Reincarnation

**Alignment:** LG
**Capital:** Sangpo-Jong (20,340)
**Notable Settlements:**
Babschu-Jong (15,320),
Byangshar-Jong (10,900), Dogul-Jong (8,440)
**Ruler:** Gyaltho Tulku (LG male samsaran cleric of Tsukiyo 20)
**Government:** Secular autocracy appointed by ruling theocrats
**Major Races:** Samsarans, Tian-Las (also giants, hobgoblins, Tian-Mins, Tian-Shus, and fiendish troglodytes)
**Languages:** Giant, Hon-La, Samsaran, Tien
**Religion:** Pharasma, Qi Zhong, Shelyn, Shizuru, Tsukiyo, Yamatsumi
**Resources:** Artwork, gems, herbs, incense, livestock, stone

The mountain nation of Zi Ha is a land of contrasts. A realm of spiritual enlightenment, monastic study, and tranquility, these mountains are the ancestral home of the samsaran race. Yet the Zi Ha Mountains also harbor vast stretches of bleak, unforgiving terrain populated by bizarre giants, savage cannibal tribes, and fiendish monsters found nowhere else in Tian Xia. Each mountain in the range can be classified into one of three categories. The Enlightened Peaks are those under the direct control of the samsaran nation—these peaks tend to be focused in the southern end, but extend most of the way up the center of the range. The Savage Peaks are those under the control of brutish giants, barbaric cannibals, and outcast hobgoblin tribes—these peaks tend to be in the north or along the eastern and western lowlands bordering Kaoling and Chu Ye. The Wild Peaks are those claimed only by monsters and wildlife—these peaks can be found throughout the range, but many lie in the lowlands bordering Jinin and Wanshou. The mountains themselves are often snowcapped, with the highest peaks reaching heights of just over 15,000 feet—a significant range, yet one that is dwarfed by the Wall of Heaven.

While Zi Ha was never directly under the rule of Lung Wa, the land enjoyed relatively peaceful relations with the people of that empire. Distance and inaccessibility played a strong role in Lung Wa's disinterest in direct control of the mountains. Like islands in a vast and treacherous sea, the great cities of Zi Ha tend to be located near the peaks of mountains, with the majority of the squat, well-constructed stone pagodas being located on the leeward side of the mountains. These cities are connected by well-maintained roads that allow for easy travel through the Enlightened Peaks. Known collectively as *jongs* (a samsaran word that means safety, shelter, and settlement), these cities function

primarily as administrative and mercantile centers rather than true bastions of force, with the valleys deep between the Enlightened Peaks being protected not by defenders, but by fortifications and obfuscating magic that hides them from sight and confuses outsiders with illusions and warding enchantments. Beyond these hidden places, the mountains themselves are deadly and unforgiving, but filled with rare herbs and untapped veins of gold and gemstones that often tempt visitors into their wilds.

Zi Ha interacts little with its neighbors except for trade, and its people rarely leave the mountains they consider holy. The lack of young children among the largely samsaran cities often unnerves visitors, but there is nothing sinister about this strange feature, for samsarans who give birth do so to human offspring, who are sent away to live with their fellow humans. When a samsaran gives birth to a child, the newborn is either escorted by its parents into a neighboring human land (typically Amanandar) to be raised as one of them, or is entrusted to one of dozens of regular long-distance caravans that link trade between Zi Ha and distant nations.

**City of Bone and Juniper:** Bizarre as they are territorial, the taiga giants of Zi Ha claim to be the offspring of an underworld dragon and an ancient samsaran noble who sought to escape the cycle of rebirth and remain in the world with her. The giants worship their mother's bones within a golden mausoleum atop a hidden plateau marked by three great towers of wood and bones. The giants usually dress in red and black, and attack on sight, dragging away any dead and their treasures alike. Oddly, at other times they dress in mottled blue and white (their mother's color) and peacefully descend to trade with human and samsaran villages, obeying a strict code of silence when they do.

**Labyrinth of the Two Hells:** The caves known as the Labyrinth of the Two Hells are an extensive and perpetual war zone between two equally brutal tribes of Hell-tainted reptilians. At war with one another in and under the southern mountains of Zi Ha are the fiendish gugrangmyal and gutshadmyal, the "children of the cold hell" and the "children of the hot hell." Both species are fiendish troglodytes, but their otherworldly ancestry is the subject of many unverified rumors.

**Sangpo-Jong:** The capital of Zi Ha, Sangpo-Jong, nominally rules over the entire samsaran nation, though the smaller cities retain considerable autonomy. Restricted to natives and those outsiders granted access, Sangpo-Jong is a place of wonder. Entry is gained by way of staircases carved into the mountains, decorated with a progression of twisting carvings of great dragons, starting with the underworld dragon at the stair's base, then sovereign dragons, and finally sky dragons at the summit, a motif repeated heavily in samsaran culture.

## LOST EMPIRES

Tian Xia has been populated by humanity for approximately 7,000 years, yet only for the past 4,000 or so have the great Tian empires ruled. Some of these early empires, like Xa Hoi, still exist today, but the most powerful of them have come and gone. Brief notes on several of the more significant of these ancient empires are given below. Other empires and countries have risen and fallen over the ages, but very few of them have left quite as significant a legacy as the ones detailed below. The map on the facing page indicates the extent of these empires at their height.

**Lung Wa:** Established in 6642 IC, Lung Wa rose from the ashes of the empire of Shu after a 106-year period of chaos, anarchy, and war. While Yixing lasted longer and Shu was larger, historians agree that Lung Wa was the most successful of the three Great Empires. It enjoyed the longest periods of peace and accomplished the greatest deeds, but certain scholars argue that Lung Wa's perceived "greatness" is an illusion, and its accomplishments seem grander because of their recency. Lung Wa's collapse in 7106 IC came as a terrible shock to Tian Xia, for very little seemed to forecast such trouble. That this collapse happened in the same year that other great calamities shook Golarion (including the death of Aroden, the formation of the Eye of Abendego, and the devastating storms that swept across the planet) has intrigued many, but no concrete link to those events has yet surfaced. Historians have noted that the distance in time between Shu's fall and Lung Wa's rise is close to being eclipsed by the period between Lung Wa's fall and the rise of the next empire in mainland Tian Xia. That no single Successor State seems poised to rebuild itself and achieve supremacy has some believing that the time of the great empires is well and truly over—but just as many scholars and philosophers take this as evidence that a new empire may be very close to uniting Tian Xia once again.

**Shu:** The empire of Shu was the largest but shortest-lived of the mainland Tian Xia empires. After Yixing's fall in 5576 IC, the mainland teetered on the edge of a devastating anarchy before the Shu managed to bring civilization back. This imperial family was so beloved that the people took their name as their own—the Tian-Shu ethnicity remains as a legacy even today to the success of this empire. Shu collapsed in 6536 IC in an even greater fall than Yixing—this time, however, the mainland would endure many years of chaos before emerging into the empire of Lung Wa.

**Taumata:** This legendary civilization of dark-skinned humans once united southern Tian Xia with the mysterious continent of Sarusan. An ancient catastrophe of unknown source destroyed this empire long before the first Tians came south into the Wandering Isles of Minata—only strange remnants from the empire of Taumata remain today, and those remnants are notoriously difficult to reach because of their isolation in southern Minata.

**Teikoku:** Sometimes referred to today as the First Kingdom of Minkai, the Teikoku Shogunate rose in 2612 IC, and continued to rule the peninsula after Shizuru granted the Teikoku family the right to rule above the empire's other four imperial families. These four families became known, collectively, as the Minkai ("great rulers"), with the Teikoku family itself taking the honor as Daiminkai over the other four. The Minkai were content to serve the Shogunate for 3,000 years, for the Teikoku were well known to be honorable and fair. Yet when corruption among the Daiminkai grew so blatant that it could no longer be ignored, the Perfect Swordswoman Setsuna Kuga led the armies of the Minkai against the Shogunate at the Battle of Eight Bridges in 6116 IC. The empire of Minkai rose swiftly after that, with a humbled Teikoku family abandoning the title of Daiminkai and joining the other four families in a shared rule of the peninsula, finally ruling in the way Shizuru had intended after thousands of years of rule under a single, all-powerful shogun.

**Valashai:** The mysterious empire of Valashai predated the arrival of humanity on Tian Xia by thousands of years—by all estimates, this truly ancient empire was a contemporary of Azlant, although there is no evidence to support the idea that there was any contact between the two civilizations. Valashai itself sprawled along Tian Xia's southern extent, and is remembered today in the word "Valashmai." Few ruins from Valashai survive today, and those that do are well hidden and remote in the dangerous extents of the Valashmai Jungle. What does seem apparent is that the Valashaians were reptilian and two to three times the size of humans—whether or not any of these mysterious ancients still live in some hidden retreat in or under the Valashmai Jungle is unknown.

**Yixing:** This empire was the first and, to date, the longest lasting of the three Great Empires that have united mainland Tian Xia over the millennia, and its founding ushered in a new age of prosperity and innovation for the entire region. The empire of Yixing made first contact with the Inner Sea, and many of the empire's traditions (such as tea ceremonies, martial arts, and philosophies like Pao-Lung and Sangpotshi) have continued to shape Tian Xia to this very day. This empire ruled for over 5,500 years, from 1 IC to 5576 IC, although it wasn't until over midway through its existence, in 3020 IC, that Yixing truly became a continent-spanning empire.

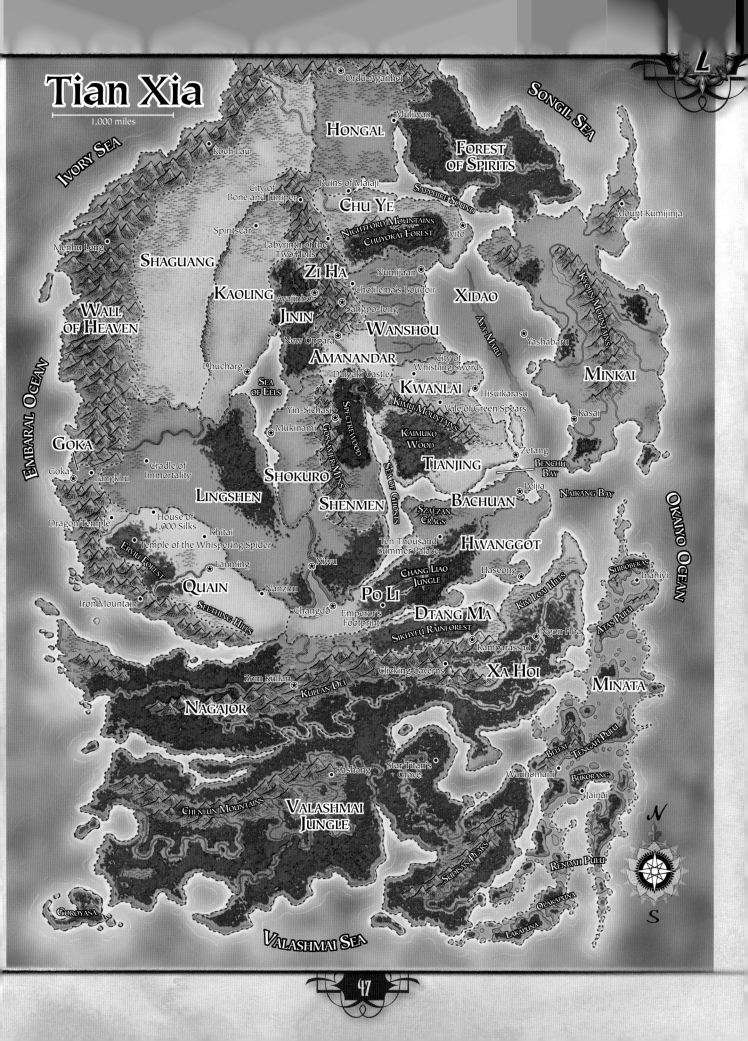

# Tian Xia

1,000 miles

IVORY SEA

SONGIL SEA

HONGAL

Ordu-Aganhei

Muliwan

FOREST OF SPIRITS

Koch Tau

Ruins of Maiaji

Mount Kumijinja

City of Bone and Juniper

CHU YE

SAPPHIRE SOUND

Spiritscar

NIGHTFORD MOUNTAINS

CHUYOKAI FOREST

Iyito

Menhu Leng

Labyrinth of the Two Hells

SHAGUANG

ZI HA

Numijaan

XIDAO

Chotilema's Boudoir

KAOLING

Ayajinbo

Sangpo-Jong

WALL OF HEAVEN

JININ

WANSHOU

KYONIN MOUNTAINS

New Oppara

Yashabaru

MINKAI

Dhucharg

AMANANDAR

City of Whistling Swords

Daigaki Castle

KWANLAI

Hisuikarasu

SEA OF EELS

Yin-Sichasi

KINJU MOUNTAINS

Vale of Green Spears

Kasai

Mukinami

KAIMUKO WOOD

GOKA

SHOKURO

TIANJING

Zetang

Goka

Langkhu

SHENMEN

BENCHU BAY

Cradle of Immortality

Peijia

LINGSHEN

SZALEZAN CRAGS

BACHUAN

NAIKANG BAY

Dragon Temple

House of 1,000 Silks

Khitai

Ten Thousand Summer Palace

HWANGGOT

SHIBOBEKAS

Temple of the Whispering Spider

Xiwu

Haseong

Inahiyi

Lanming

CHANG LIAO JUNGLE

KIM LOAI HILLS

QUAIN

Nanzhu

PO LI

Ngon Hoa

Iron Mountain

Changdo

Emperor's Footprint

DTANG MA

Ramparassad

SIKHYEU RAINFOREST

SEETHING HILLS

Clicking Caverns

XA HOI

MINATA

Zom Kullan

KULLAN DEI

BELEM

TENGAH PULU

NAGAJOR

Bukorang

Waunomani

Jainai

Kashang

Star Titan's Grave

CHENLUN MOUNTAINS

VALASHMAI JUNGLE

RENDAH PULU

SUDISAN PEAKS

GOROYASA

OLAKAPUNA

VALASHMAI SEA

LAKAPUNA

EMBARAL OCEAN

OKAIYO OCEAN

ATAS PULU

SEA OF GHOSTS

GOSSAMER MTNS

SPECTREWOOD

ERYIU FOREST

AXA-MARU

N

S

# Life in the Dragon Empires

Look around you, friend. We have many gods, and those gods fill many functions. The gods of this province alone have lessons enough for all of our lifetimes. Each depiction of the divine tells a story, and when we look upon these murals and statues with the eyes of a sage, we see the true meaning of divinity. These small details, they tell a true story and point us toward a higher truth. If we are brave, or if we are wise, or if we leave behind a legend, we may join them. It is through the study of our gods that we become better people. It is through them that we achieve divinity ourselves.

—Tuyet An Hoi, priest of Irori

Humanity has been the dominant race of Tian Xia for ages. And in those ages, dynasties have emerged and fallen, cities have risen and crumbled, and empires have spread and collapsed. And they shall continue to do so into the foreseeable future—indeed, for many Dragon Empire philosophers, grasping the concept of the cycle of incarnation, be it of life or nation or thought, is fundamental to understanding history, the future, and the now. What is only is because it was and will be again someday—a circular bit of logic nonetheless popular among this land's scholars.

This attitude makes it possible to understand the enormity of the more recent history of the Dragon Empires: Nearly an entire continent had been ruled by one empire, Lung Wa, until it suddenly collapsed on itself, giving rise to dozens of independent nations, each vying, it seems, to be the new ruler of the Dragon Empires. Lung Wa is far from the first continental empire in this land to rise and fall. It will not be the last. Yet for hundreds of years, Lung Wa had sculpted the shape of the nations, forcing its culture upon its subjects, renaming their countries and their customs, and stamping out the individuality of the people as a whole where it found them. In fact, the continental name "Tian Xia" arises from the language of Lung Wa and the empires that preceeded it, as do many common names of the other cultures of this land—a usage that has rooted itself deep into the histories of their subjects. Even though Lung Wa no longer exists as a physical empire, traces of it thus remain on the lips of all who dwell within its echo. But throughout the ages, regardless of which empire's influence prevailed, the land has been known as the Dragon Empires.

To define Tians collectively as the result of these conquests would be to ignore the whole story, however. The Dragon Empires are a place where myth, legend, and reality share space equally in daily life, and while the appearance of the supernatural may be a cause for alarm or celebration, it rarely comes as a surprise. Shrines to household spirits fill the houses across the Dragon Empires, and roadside temples run a brisk trade in cures, exorcisms, and appeasements to the spirits that fill the land. Everywhere, the boundaries between the fantastical and the mundane are blurry—if indeed they exist at all.

The people and the land share a connection that they welcome wholeheartedly. This connection is both brutal and loving, one that inspires devotion even as it gives rise to the fatalism that allows Tians to weather the fury of nature. Those who move to the cities in search of security, wealth, or glory express a longing for the places they left behind, and though they may choose to ignore their pasts, they cannot deny the yearning for their homes in their hearts. Even those who have rejected rural life idealize it in their music, their art, and their poetry. Art is important to most Tians, for each new piece of art created enhances the world all the more. Whether through the written word—either the grace of prose or poetry or the gentle but demanding art of calligraphy—or through painting or architecture or weaving or music—from the crashing taiko to the hypnotic sound of the shamisen—the Tians treat the expression of art as one of the great treasures of the land, and they honor artists above many others.

Much of the Tians' appreciation for art stems from their philosophies, which root them in the here and now while allowing them to dream huge dreams. In the Inner Sea, many monarchies have rooted themselves in the divine right of kings to rule. In Tian Xia, people may believe in the divinity of their rulers themselves, not by decree but by personal experience, knowing that it is possible to have one's life assigned by the fates. They see the samsarans of Zi Ha returning in life after life. They witness the supernatural creatures of the Forest of Spirits, the strange monsters from the southern jungles, and the world-shaking power of the Imperial Dragons, and they make room for these in their worldviews.

Yet do not assume that Tians' love of art and deep philosophical traditions have resulted in a utopian society. Quite the opposite, for one person's art is another's rubbish, and one person's philosophy is another's heresy. Wars have sparked in the Dragon Empires over disparaging comments about paintings or minor differences in philosophical interpretations of the stars or seas. One need look only at the continent's history to see proof of this, for the Dragon Empires have forged a pattern of vast kingdoms and dynasties rising to rule the entire land for centuries at a stroke, only to collapse and throw the land into chaos. Such an advent of dissolution recently struck with the fall of Imperial Lung Wa, and today the Dragon Empires once again consist of dozens of different nations, each eager to pick up the mantle of rule, yet just as eager in many cases that their neighbors do not. Such is the way of things in the Dragon Empires, where individuals are not the only entities to follow the path of death and reincarnation—for empires themselves can rise from the ashes and rule again.

## LANGUAGES OF TIAN XIA

The people of the Dragon Empires speak many languages, from the widespread Tien to the nearly forgotten tongues of lost kingdoms.

### MODERN HUMAN LANGUAGES

The following are the most common human languages spoken in the Dragon Empires.

**Dtang:** This is the language of Dtang Ma and the native tongue of the Tian-Dtang people. It is spoken primarily in southeastern Tian Xia.

**Hon-La:** The Tian-Las speak Hon-La. This language is typically spoken in northern Tian Xia, particularly in Hongal and Shaguang.

**Hwan:** The Tian-Hwan people of Hwanggot speak Hwan. This language is spoken primarily in Hwanggot, but also sees much use among resistance fighters who traditionally opposed Lung Wa's regime (and those who now oppose Successor States attempting to claim parts of Lung Wa)—an irony, perhaps, given Hwanggot's traditions of peace.

**Kelish:** The language of the Padishah Empire of Kelesh in the west, Kelish is often spoken in Goka as a sort of trade tongue by merchants.

**Minatan:** The Wandering Isles feature countless isolated tribes, many of whom speak distinct but closely related tongues. The Minatan language is a combination of these tongues—one who speaks Minatan can generally communicate with most of Minata's people. Minatan is spoken most often in southeastern Tian Xia.

**Minkaian:** One of the most widespread of human languages in Tian Xia, Minkaian is the native tongue of the Tian-Min. It is spoken in Minkai and throughout northern and central Tian Xia, particularly in regions like Jinin, Shokuro, Chu Ye, and Wanshou.

**Senzar:** This language was old even when humanity first rose in the Dragon Empires. Senzar is the language of the ancient spirits of the land—it is often associated with kami and the Forest of Spirits, but many denizens of the Wall of Heaven speak it as well. Senzar may be the original source of the various human tongues, for many Senzar words, particularly ones associated with the spirit world or dragons, resemble their counterparts in modern languages.

**Taldane:** The so-called "common tongue" of the Inner Sea region is spoken in parts of Tian Xia, particularly in the north and west where trade with those distant lands is more common. Taldane is also the official tongue of the nation of Amanandar, and its influence is slowly spreading into all nations that neighbor this small but powerful kingdom.

**Tien:** Once the official language of Lung Wa, Tien is the most widespread of the continent's languages, and is the one most commonly found beyond the Dragon Empires' borders. It remains the official language of many mainland nations, and is spoken in all nations as a trade tongue. Tien is the language of choice if one wishes to speak and be heard anywhere in the Dragon Empires.

**Vudrani:** Vudrani is perhaps the most widespread foreign tongue in Tian Xia. Speakers of this tongue are most common in southwestern Tian Xia, and in the city of Goka.

## OTHER LANGUAGES

Beyond human tongues, several other languages are quite common in certain reaches of the Dragon Empires.

**Abyssal:** The language of demons, Abyssal is often spoken by oni and other evil spirits.

**Aklo:** This ancient tongue is spoken by the denizens of the Darklands, strange eldritch entities, and certain ancient intruders from the First World.

**Aquan:** The so-called "tongue of the sea" is spoken primarily in the sunken nation of Xidao by the locathahs—those who trade frequently with the ocean empires often speak this tongue as well.

**Auran:** This soft-spoken, breathy language, the "tongue of the heavens," is spoken most often in the mountainous regions of the world, particularly Zi Ha and the Wall of Heaven.

**Celestial:** The language of angels, Celestial is the official national tongue of Tianjing, but is slowly gaining influence in Kwanlai.

**Draconic:** The language of dragons is known throughout the land, but has its strongest representation in the nation of Xa Hoi.

**Druidic:** Druids are rather rare in the Dragon Empires—most who speak this tongue are foreigners traveling from the Inner Sea region.

**Elven:** The official tongue of Jinin, Elven is also relatively common in Kaoling, Zi Ha, Shokuro, and Amanandar.

**Giant:** This brutish tongue and its numerous minor variants are spoken most often in Chu Ye today, but are of use in any region where the wrath of giants is known.

**Goblin:** The official language of hobgoblin-ruled Kaoling, this dialect is similar to the Goblin tongue spoken elsewhere in the world. The goblin-speaking people of the Dragon Empires use the Tien alphabet when utilizing the written form.

**Ignan:** The "tongue of fire" is spoken most often in central Nagajor and the mountains of Valashmai.

**Infernal:** The language of devils is often spoken by oni and other evil spirits.

**Nagaji:** This hissing tongue is the national language of Nagajor, but is spoken throughout the Dragon Empires.

**Necril:** An ancient language of the dead, this whispering tongue is shared among undead throughout Golarion, and is also often associated with necromancy.

**Samsaran:** The official tongue of Zi Ha and the samsaran race, this language is spoken throughout the Dragon Empires.

**Sylvan:** The language of the fey is known but uncommon in Tian Xia—most of the creatures one would expect to speak this language instead speak Senzar.

**Tengu:** The official language of Kwanlai and the tongue of the tengu race, this language is spoken throughout the Dragon Empires.

**Terran:** The "tongue of earth" is spoken most often in the Darklands.

**Undercommon:** This language, derived from an ancient combination of Elven and even older tongues, is spoken throughout the Darklands.

**Wayang:** The racial tongue of the wayang is spoken throughout the Dragon Empires, but most often in the Wandering Isles of Minata.

## THE DRAGON EMPIRES ZODIAC

It is said in the Dragon Empires that the stars guide the lives of all who dwell beneath their light. Whether they are deities, spirits, demons, dragons, or mortal beings (for accounts vary among the people of the land), the constellations of the sky are said to lay out a path for every mortal to tread. Each year, a new constellation becomes ascendant in the night sky, and within that year, constellations rise and fall by the month and hour, influencing new souls and overseeing their charges.

These influences in the night sky take particular notice of those born under their signs, granting indications of their favor and gifting these mortals with the strength of the guardians. It is believed that the imperial dragons of the land are the guardians of the zodiac, and certainly all five species of these wyrms are represented in the constellations. The people of the Dragon Empires offer propitiation to the stars when embarking on a task under the gaze or the purview of these watchmen.

Many Tians use the zodiac to mark the progression of the years, months, and hours of the day. Further, the time and date of a person's birth (night and day being irrelevant, despite the fact that the stars are only visible at night) are invariably tied to one of the constellations of the zodiac—it is believed that these influences combine to create tremendous differences in personality and destiny. The primary constellations and the attributes they are said to impart to those born under their sign are as follows.

**The Underworld Dragon:** This constellation is also called the Guardian; those born under this sign are tenacious, foresighted, and industrious, but can be secretive, brooding, and cold.

**The Swordswoman:** In some cultures, they call her the Warrior. Her children are resolute, daring, and charismatic, but they can be foolhardy, hot-tempered, and opportunistic.

**The Sea Dragon:** The sea-folk call him Father Ocean, and his wards are gracious, generous, and vigorous; they are also tempestuous, brash, and fickle.

**The Swallow:** The bird varies by culture, possibly becoming Hawk, Eagle, or Egret, but is always female. Those born under this sign are alert, sociable, and agile. Their detractors call them flighty, impetuous, and argumentative.

**The Ox:** Tian-Dtangs and Tian-Hwans also call him the Water Buffalo. The children of the Ox are dependable, honest, and stolid, but can be inflexible, narrow minded, and angry.

**The Sovereign Dragon:** The Empress's steady hand offers calm, charisma, and nobility to her children, but they are also known to be arrogant, demanding, and manipulative.

**The Ogre:** Though the Ogre is typically a monster, the constellation that bears his name is an aloof guardian that is not inherently evil. His children are strong, self-sufficient, and daring, but can likewise be selfish, aggressive, and solitary.

**The Forest Dragon:** Those born under the Forest Dragon are shrewd, cautious, and sensual, but can be dishonest, vengeful, and remote.

**The Blossom:** Also called the Cherry Tree. Those of the Blossom are beautiful, artistic, and insightful but can be fragile, egotistic, and driven.

**The Dog:** Those born under the sign of the Dog are friendly, loyal, and optimistic, but they can also be lazy, aggressive, and gluttonous.

**The Sky Dragon:** Those the Lord of the Sky guides are intellectual, graceful, and foresighted, but like their namesake, these people can be distrustful, disdainful, and over-sensitive.

**The Archer:** Also called the Breath. Her children are observant, patient, and self-assured, but can be self-indulgent, distant, and jealous.

## SOCIETY

Life in the Dragon Empires differs dramatically depending upon where you find yourself and who you are. The streets of Goka are generally welcoming of any race, but anyone other than an aasimar would find it difficult being accepted and taken seriously in Tianjing. The gardens of Hwanggot are peaceful and serene, a stark contrast to the ruins and violence of Chu Ye's devastated cities. Yet regardless of situation, location, and race, certain elements of life in the Dragon Empires cleave to central standards and themes, as explored in the following pages.

### TRADE AND COINS

Though the great empire of Lung Wa has collapsed, trade continues. Indeed, the system of commerce established in the Dragon Empires is said to flow through any storm, and the rise of trade in the wake of Lung Wa's end only proves this. Since the Dragon Empires are still struggling to find their new face and place even more than a century after the fall of Lung Wa, most cities eagerly accept coinage of any mint, and the standardization of coins along the copper, silver, and gold denominations has become commonplace, perhaps due to the international influence of the great city of Goka.

The coinage of Lung Wa continues to be legal tender throughout much of the land of the Dragon Empires. Originally based on the design of rare and beautiful shells (the original currency of Tian Xia), the coins of Lung

Wa have changed in shape and size but retain signifiers that indicate their history. Minted under the guidance of imperial coin makers, the currency is bent and shaped precisely to resemble the curve of a shell, allowing the coins to be stacked atop each other easily. Square holes punched through the center of each coin allow people to thread the coins together, and approximately 600 coins can fit on a yard of string. The primary metal of these coins is silver, though lower denominations are made of copper. Gold coins are far more rare, with platinum coins being the rarest of all; most rulers demand that any platinum coins in circulation be returned to the central banks of their nations. Since the collapse of Lung Wa, experiments with cloth and paper money have largely ended, and stashes of such experimental currencies are all but valueless these days.

Trade continues to be essential, however, even in these uncertain times, and barter remains a common tactic when coinage fails. The rice from Wanshou is crucial to the diets of much of the rest of the continent. Wheat from Amanandar travels far. The iron ingots of the mines of Lingshen are made into Po Lian swords and Hwan plowshares. Wood and jade travel from one end of the continent to the other. Through the changing borders, trade caravans continue to roll and merchant ships continue to sail.

## NATIONAL CONFLICTS

Despite the valiant attempts of some (particularly Hwanggot and Tianjing), none of the countries of Tian Xia are in a state of complete peace at any given moment. The fall of Lung Wa at the onset of the Age of Succession opened the door to chaos, and despite the passage of over a hundred years, that chaos remains strong. Many of the Successor States vie to gain control of the *Five Dragon Throne* in Po Li and so stamp their authority on their rivals, and their agents travel the breadth of the continent to seek advantage over the others. The empire of Minkai began the Age of Succession in a strong position, and had it not soon succumbed to internal strife and trouble, it could well have become the new dominant empire in the land. Instead, today Minkai teeters on the edge of civil war as its Jade Regent grows more and more demanding of and abusive toward his subjects. The Zo pirates of Minata increasingly cause trouble in the shipping lanes off the eastern coastline, and enemy nations occasionally fly the flag of Minata so that they might engage in bloodshed without provoking an international incident. The hobgoblins of Kaoling prey on the weak and hungry, and make frequent raids across the borders of Lingshen, Jinin, and Zi Ha. Likewise, the nation of Chu Ye pushes against its borders, though internal fighting prevents it from making full-scale assaults. Dtang Ma tries its best to keep from being sucked into these conflicts, but will likely fail. In Amanandar, the Taldans fight a defensive battle against the warlords on their borders, and occasionally push out to make a land grab against an enemy who has become too aggressive.

The nations fight hidden battles, as well—not all wars are won on the battlefield. Teams of assassins roam the rooftops and alleyways of cities, striking down leaders and powers behind the thrones. Fluctuations in currency and manipulations of the great markets of Goka have brought some nations' economies to their knees. Intrigues and conspiracies are a fact of life, and behind the painted face of a courtier lies the soul of a demon. Spies and betrayal are a fact of life; indeed, in certain strata of society, the occupation of spy is highly regarded. The word "peace" between the nations of Tian Xia means only that they engage in the careful and courtly dance of diplomacy, a slow war for advantage so that the fast war for blood need not arise. Though they may be allies, alliances stretch only so far.

## BIRTHRIGHTS AND FAMILY

One's birth is a blood gift—a gift known as *sangpotshi*. A person's sangpotshi is a representation of her karma and fate, determined not only by her parents' honor and station, but by the influence of her past lives, if any. By living according to the needs of their sangpotshi, Tians hope to live a blameless life so as to be born again in a better station in the next. Though many Tians might not accept the exact tenets of the philosophy of sangpotshi, few believe in "accidents of birth." Thus, those born into nobility or royalty are considered favored of the gods, with revolt and treason seen as revolt against those who have striven to be better people. Such acts are viewed as shameful blights on honor and attacks against the word of Fate—unless they succeed, in which case such acts are the work of destiny. Only the blooded of the land are allowed this latitude, for the nobles and those born to great destinies have little reason to wish things different. Ironically, this means that great change, when it comes to the Dragon Empires, tends to come not from its leaders but from individuals who must strive to be noticed and heard all their lives.

While loyalty to one's ruler or deity is important, family is perhaps the most important unit across all the cultures of Tian Xia. The study of genealogy is a much-respected pursuit, with most rulers employing small armies of genealogists who constantly study their families' ancestry. Since one's possible triumphs in life are believed to be manipulated and influenced not only by one's past lives and karma but by the influence of one's ancestors working upon sangpotshi, knowledge of family history is of great import to Tians. Those who cannot or will not provide information about their families are

often the object of suspicion and distrust. Thus, any who are unable to provide exacting details (and accompanying proof) of their lineage and ancestry find it difficult or impossible to achieve true positions of power—yet it is from such unknowns that many of the Dragon Empires' greatest heroes and villains have risen.

## City Life in the Dragon Empires

For the lower class in urban environs, life is dirty. Charged with keeping the cities clean and habitable, this class includes the servants and beggars. They and their families live in rented apartments packed closely together. Their food is usually a handful of rice and fish, or noodles with chicken stock. Members of this class are crucial to the functioning of society, but they are not welcome in it. They have little of the breeding and reserve of their betters, and so they are more able to express their natural humanity—in games of chance, in drinking and drugs, and in their personal appearance.

The middle class (artisans, merchants, mid-level priests, highly skilled tradesmen, bureaucrats, and government functionaries) see the city as a necessary place for the practice of their livelihoods. They live in more durable dwellings on safer streets, and seek to be as cosmopolitan as possible in all their dealings. If they came to the city with an accent, they seek to eradicate it as quickly as possible. They keep themselves appraised of the latest news and fashions, hoping that they will be noticed and elevated more quickly thereby. Because of this, they are occasionally swept into heresies that they later regret. Their foods and pleasures are more refined, yet still limited by income.

Nobility can afford to live where they choose—and where they choose to live tends to change to match their needs. Proximity to the lower and middle class is required, for these classes exist mostly to ensure nobility can live in comfort. The stereotype of the noble who doesn't think of the "help" as even being people exists for a reason—exceptions certainly exist, with some nobles taking better care of the lower classes, but by and large the aristocracy of a city are loath to mix with those of lower breeding.

## Rural Life in the Dragon Empires

The life of a rural peasant in the Dragon Empires is much like the life of a peasant anywhere on Golarion: short, tedious, and occasionally interrupted by horrors and wonders. Rural Tian society from north to south and east to west relies strongly on familial ties. It is not uncommon for four generations to live under the same roof in a house that has stood for hundreds of years, rebuilt after natural disasters like volcanoes, tsunamis, earthquakes, or floods, or after man-made disasters like wars. Part of the reason Tians have developed such a formal manner of speech is because of the complex web of interrelationships within families that spread out over time, with other families of the village, and with families of other villages. Each person within this system must know her place and the place of others, and it is far better to err on the side of civility and formality than to suffer the wrath of an insulted guest.

Though over the millennia, countless farms and cities have been plowed under, turned to dust, or destroyed by battles, little generally changes in villagers' lives from day to day. Farmers, hunters, and the like rise before dawn to trudge to their work, expecting each day to be much like the ones before, with only a handful of cold rice or yesterday's dinner to feed them. If their work takes them far from their homes, they pack themselves seasonal fruit or a lunch prepared by family members who must remain at home. The arrival of a traveling aristocrat or government official is always a big event, often resulting in an entire village dropping everything to focus on making the visitor's stay as memorable and pleasant as possible, for when that noble returns to the city, she may have kind words to say of the villagers. And in the long term, such kind words can yield a greater return to the eager peasants than any amount of coin.

## Yokai and the Spirit World

As any native of Tian Xia can tell you, city life and rural life are but two elements of the trinity of existence in the Dragon Empires. The third element is, perhaps, the most important, for the *yokai* of the spirit world wield great power to manipulate the very rules of creation. The term "yokai" is believed to come from Minkai, but has since spread throughout Tian Xia to represent all creatures of the supernatural, be they benevolent kami or destructive oni, minor ghosts or overwhelming dragons. Superstition is a powerful, almost palpable force among the people of Tian Xia, as one might expect in a nation where the strange and otherworldly often interact directly with everyday workings of life. Even those who do not follow local beliefs see the everyday influence of spirits in their lives. Tian Xia is a haunted land, a place where the dead do not hurry to their appointed places and where one's ancestors might watch over the clan to protect and guide it through troubled times. The lowest peasant and the greatest king thus seek to appease the yokai, calling on allies in the world beyond for guidance and aid. These spirits need not be those of the dead, however—nature spirits and spirits called forth from the skill of artisans are common too, dwelling in places of natural beauty and cunning handiwork.

Just as the word "yokai" comes from Minkai, so too has the practice of erecting ornate, often freestanding gates known as *torii* spread throughout the Dragon Empires. These ornate gateways are said to guard the boundaries between the mortal world and the spirit world, from whence

the yokai and practicers of magic gain their supernatural power. Torii just as often serve to warn travelers of the presence of spiritual or yokai activity in a region as they do to honor and appease the whims of local ghosts and legends. Often incorporated into the walls of important structures or the divisions between cities, but just as often rising in the middle of a field or lost in the depths of a forest, torii can be of any color but are most often some shade of red, for it is believed that red holds the greatest attraction to the yokai. Torii are traditionally made of wood or stone, but they can be made of any material found in abundance. Most torii do not have any innate powers, yet some torii are magical in nature and bear many strange powers, ranging from the ability to heal or harm those who pass through to serving as portals for swift travel between nations or worlds.

## THE ROLE OF MAGIC

Magic is a fundamental part of society in the Dragon Empires, and is often seen as the right of those in power. Yet just as often, because of the whim of sangpotshi, even lowborn peasants or ragged slaves can find in themselves the potential for the use of magic. The people of the Dragon Empires know life can be hard, and that magic can ease many of life's pains. Yet magic is also a source of distrust and worry, for as the wise are fond of pointing out, magic merely enhances and strengthens the innate qualities of the world—and when the world is a cruel place, so is its magic. As a result, many governments seek to regulate or control the use of magic, for in the hands of a single embittered peasant or ambitious bandit, magic can wreak as much havoc on the order of society as any army or rampaging monster. Spellcasters are often expected to register their gifts and talents with the government, with the implied assumption that should their talents be needed for the defense of the nation or the entertainment of its lords, spellcasters must be ready to serve as required.

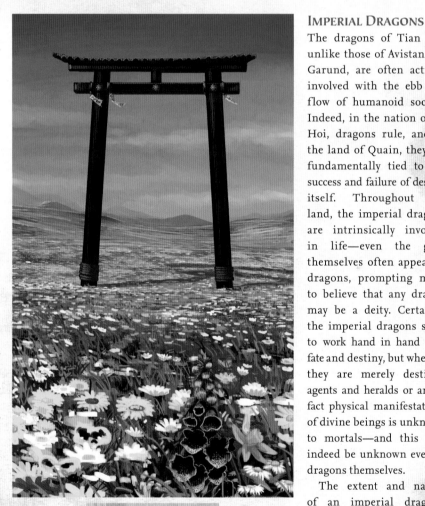

**TORII GATE**

Of course, in some parts of Tian Xia, magic plays an even more central role in life. Places like the Forest of Spirits, the Wall of Heaven, or the Valashmai Jungle teem with magic, both in the form of powerful yokai and strange supernatural forces. Other regions, such as Chu Ye or Dtang Ma, are ruled by those who have mastered the intricacies of magic, be it for the weal or woe of their subjects.

## IMPERIAL DRAGONS

The dragons of Tian Xia, unlike those of Avistan and Garund, are often actively involved with the ebb and flow of humanoid society. Indeed, in the nation of Xa Hoi, dragons rule, and in the land of Quain, they are fundamentally tied to the success and failure of destiny itself. Throughout the land, the imperial dragons are intrinsically involved in life—even the gods themselves often appear as dragons, prompting many to believe that any dragon may be a deity. Certainly, the imperial dragons seem to work hand in hand with fate and destiny, but whether they are merely destiny's agents and heralds or are in fact physical manifestations of divine beings is unknown to mortals—and this may indeed be unknown even to dragons themselves.

The extent and nature of an imperial dragon's involvement with any given society is detailed for each of the regions, and can vary from being a fundamental part of that society to being nonexistent. Regardless, imperial dragons tend to be more active in times of great upheaval—although they can be slow to react to such changes. It's taken the imperial dragons of the empires nearly a century to react fully to the fall of Lung Wa, for example—but now, one need not look far in the Dragon Empires to see the influence of the continent's namesakes upon the cities and wildlands of the world.

Five varieties of imperial dragons exist—rules for the five are presented in *Pathfinder RPG Bestiary 3*.

# DRAGON EMPIRE FACTIONS

Certain groups and organizations in the Dragon Empires carry with them greater power and notoriety than any single religion or nation—in fact, these factions often embrace members from multiple nations or several religions, each drawing under its philosophical banner a wide range of beliefs and backgrounds. Some few factions, such as the Pathfinder Society, have a truly global presence, but those presented below are generally limited to Tian Xia. Even then, in some cases, these factions might have presences in areas beyond the Dragon Empires' borders.

**Golden League (LE):** The powerful group known as the Golden League was formed when a prominent Minkai merchant house allied itself with a notable thieves' guild in a time of desperation. The two families intertwined in shadow, and for a brief period of time near the end of the Age of Ascendency, the Golden League simultaneously controlled Minkai's legitimate markets as well as its underworld. After their manipulations of the market nearly resulted in the collapse of that empire's economy, the emperor exiled the league from Minkai and instituted several trade laws still in existence today, hoping to never again see their like. Yet this did not destroy the Golden League—after a time, they rose again on the other side of the continent in Goka. Yet they had learned from their mistakes, and now seek to manipulate trade in more subtle ways through a cagey combination of bribes, threats, and assassinations engineered to keep themselves and their allies rich. Today, the Golden League consists of dozens of different "families" in Goka who keep a presence and allies in all major cities of the Dragon Empires. No one family has complete control over the league, so if one is destroyed, the other families keep the League alive. Each of these families keeps a fighting arm of tattooed assassins and soldiers known as the "Xun," remorseless and relentless specialists in murder and intrigue. Their tattoos depict all manner of mythical monsters, but each is always surrounded in a signature shroud of flame. It is said that when one of the league's more powerful enforcers is killed, she immediately reincarnates as the creature painted on her body and fights on. Locals know to keep their heads bowed in deference when a Xun of the Golden League appears.

**Kusari-Gama (LN):** Although these monk warriors now reside in hidden dojos across Golarion, they first originated deep within the Wall of Heaven. Receiving directives from a mysterious group of monks known as the Tsu Zau Na, the Kusari-Gama are devoted to the perfection of their fighting arts as they train for a hidden war that the Tsu Zau Na believe will fall upon all of Golarion. Each individual Kusari-Gama cell pursues martial perfection in a different way, giving birth to new styles and approaches to the martial arts. Some dojos have strongly developed traditions of honor and self-sacrifice, while others are devoted to perfecting naked warfare itself, excluding mercy or restraint. The cells of Shokuro, for example, practice an art form with a mysticism that bears little resemblance to the devastating speed and strength found in Quain or the flowing styles found in the temples of Tianjing.

**Lantern Lodge (N):** The organization known as the Lantern Lodge is relatively new, but its close ties to the Pathfinder Society has ensured its swift rise in power and influence in the Dragon Empires. Although the Pathfinder Society itself is making its own expansions into Tian Xia, it is increasingly reliant on the advice and support of the Lantern Lodge. Less concerned with profiteering through the acquisition of artifacts than it is with the preservation of historical knowledge, the Lantern Lodge has found its sensibilities to be a good match for the Pathfinders. The lodge has currently begun construction of several great libraries across Tian Xia in the hope of raising interest in both the lodge itself as well as the Pathfinder Society. Many of its members master the art of calligraphy, and the Southern Tiger Lodge in Dtang Ma is rumored to be perfecting a clockwork device using stolen technology from the necropolis of Pan Majang in an attempt to replicate the wonder of the western printing press for the significantly more complex written languages of the Dragon Empires.

**Order of the Black Daimyo (LE):** Although samurai most commonly traditionally follow the order of the warrior and live lives emphasizing honor, there exist in some parts of the Dragon Empires samurai who follow more sinister teachings. These samurai are the students of General Susumu, the Black Daimyo and patron god of cruel and sadistic samurai. They also serve cruel and sadistic warlords—they are not ronin, but neither do they seek to exemplify the notions of honor and duty as those who follow the order of the warrior do. Nevertheless, samurai of the order of the Black Daimyo function as samurai of the order of the warrior—they simply replace the pursuit of honor and heroism with the pursuit of war and glory.

**Shattered Lotus (CN):** Not all are prepared to accept that Imperial Lung Wa has truly ended. The secret society of the Shattered Lotus is dedicated to rebuilding the empire and returning Tian Xia to what members believe to have been a "golden age," but that in fact more accurately translates to a Tian Xia under the rule of the Shattered Lotus. Composed of the descendants of deposed nobles, fallen monks, the children of former imperial commanders, and true believers, the Shattered Lotus seeks nothing less than the reunification of all 16 Successor States under its own rule. With a covert cell

infiltrating virtually every state in the Dragon Empire, the Shattered Lotus slowly works to enact its long-term plan. Knowing just how large the task before them truly is, members of the Shattered Lotus also know that their goals will take successive generations to achieve. Yet patience wears thin as memories of Lung Wa grow more distant and the power of the individual Successor States grows, and the Shattered Lotus increasingly turns to treachery, libel, slander, and extortion to propel nations away from peace and into war. For only when the Successor States are staggering from conflict does the Shattered Lotus feel it can rise from those ashes to reunify the Dragon Empires as its own personal empire.

**Way of the Kirin (LG):** During the height of Lung Wa's rule, the Way of the Kirin was one of the most powerful and well-funded independent military organizations in the Dragon Empires. With interests in international trade, treaties, and politics, the Way of the Kirin spread their influence as far as the Padishah Empire of Kelesh. The group itself had no central leader, but each member swore to a code of ethics that bound him to two specific causes—the support of fair economy and the opposition of corruption within all governments. The Way of the Kirin gave the common people a much-needed ally among the ruling class, and helped to ensure nobility and government did not dishonor their citizens. Alas, with Lung Wa's fall, the Way of the Kirin fell on hard times. The resulting chaos overwhelmed the organization, and many of their most powerful members were slain. Today, members of the Way of the Kirin can be found throughout Tian Xia as they work to rebuild their organization's influence.

**Wuai Ling (CE):** This fast-growing society is devoted to human supremacy. Its long-term goal is the eradication of not only monsters, but all other non-human races—or at the very least, the conquest of "inhumans" (as they are called) and relegation of races like kitsune, tengus, and samsarans to the role of slaves. The Wuai Ling often ally themselves with evil-aligned groups whose goals may be similar, but never see themselves as the subordinate in such organizations. The Wuai-Ling openly cultivate racism and promote the mistreatment of tengus, kitsune, nagaji, and the like, and often place large bounties on notable inhumans in an attempt to prevent these "lesser races" from achieving any claim of power. Nations like Kwanlai, Nagajor, Tianjing, Jinin, and Kaoling, where humanity does not rule, are seen by the Wuai Ling as the gravest threats to the Dragon Empires' future.

**Zo (CN):** Minata's largest pirate clan is filled with the ranks of the dishonored and those who have been exiled from their families. Their primary base of operation is hidden somewhere deep in Minata, a place said to be a ring-shaped island whose central harbor can be entered via the sea only by a maze of treacherous canals and straits.

Their flag, a sundered katana on a field of blood, strikes fear into the hearts of their prey, for those who have no honor have nothing to live for and are always ready to die in battle. These pirates serve as all-too-real cultural bogeymen in Minata—many parents exact obedience by threatening that children who misbehave will be sent to the Zo. The Zo's current leaders are a loose federation of ruthless pirates rumored to take instruction from a ghost ship that visits them on nights when the water is completely still.

# PHILOSOPHIES

Faith in the Dragon Empires is a strange admixture of belief, folk superstition, and the accreted ideas of healers, messiahs, and visionaries who have walked the breadth of the land over thousands of years. Tians are a pragmatic people; they take the parts of faith that work for them and discard the rest. This practice has given rise to a hodgepodge of beliefs and strange outgrowths from one end of Tian Xia to the other. Nothing prevents Tians from being adherents of these philosophies and devoted worshipers of a god; nothing about such an arrangement is strange to them. In fact, oracles often devote themselves primarily to one of the following philosophies rather than to any particular pantheon of deities.

## ICHIMEIYO

Ichimeiyo is a code for all warriors, one that stresses honor, loyalty to a cause or master, and an absolutely unbreakable will. Ichimeiyo represents the fundamental philosophical foundation for the samurai order of the warrior, but even applies to ronin who no longer serve a master. This code demands its adherents work constantly to improve themselves—and not merely through the study and constant honing of swordplay. A warrior who is mighty with the sword is still less than one who also devotes study to perfecting a garden or another who spends part of her day in meditation.

Three great precepts dominate ichimeiyo. The first is "One Body, One Soul," a directive that the initiates should strive to align their intentions with their actions. The second is "Honor Is All," for without honor, a warrior is nothing more than a savage with technique. The third is, "Without Service, Nothing": The way of the true warrior is not the way of the noble, and though nobles may walk alongside ichimeiyo, they are permitted actions that would dishonor their servants. To succeed in their study, warriors must align themselves with a master and swear loyalty. If their master dies, they must seek vengeance. If their master dishonors himself or would bring dishonor on the warriors, those sworn to that master may renounce him—and if they do not, they accept the same judgment of fate that awaits their lord.

## Pao-Lung

The teacher Pao-Lung taught of the perfectibility of mortals and the divinity of emperors. His philosophy became the basis for the state religion of Lung Wa (which is still followed to this day in Po Li), and concerned itself with the route by which dead emperors ascended to the Heavenly Bureaucracy to order the affairs of Heaven and Earth. In these teachings, the ruler is the hub around which the ruled revolve. Those who serve the emperor help to turn the wheel, the spokes of which are the relationships between courtiers and nobles, tradesmen and peasants. These relationships inspire duties and loyalties, without which the wheel will break. Even the emperor has a duty to his people, for if he cannot govern his passions, he cannot govern his people and must step aside. A virtuous ruler spreads virtue.

Thus it was that Pao-Lung presumed to teach morals to the divine. His teachings helped create a meritocracy, and they inspired a system of examinations that would allow anyone who could pass moral, physical, and mental tests to claim government posts. In turn, these posts brought honor to a family, uplifting the poor-but-wise above those who could not pass the tests. This led to schools that taught reading, writing, and moral behavior, in turn leading to education for the populace in general, and thus proved Pao-Lung correct: Mortals can improve themselves. His devotees today hold to his traditions and laws.

Yet all of this is but the base assumption of Pao-Lung's teachings, for this philosophy also speaks of how one must look to one's ancestors to see the truth of these teachings. Examples of success and failure in history live still in those memories of one's ancestors, and by honoring the ancestors and learning from them, one can engender a greater tomorrow.

## Sangpotshi, the River of Life

In the great mountains of Zi Ha, springs spill down the bluffs to create rivers, and those rivers thunder over cliffs to create waterfalls so high that little of the water reaches the ground. The water becomes vapor, returning to the river to rush over the edge again and again. So too is the endless cycle of life, for the souls of the recently dead flow like water in a metaphysical river—a river that only the most enlightened can fully traverse to reach their final reward in Pharasma's Boneyard. Most of these souls, like the water plummeting from the towering cliff, turn to vapor and are returned upriver to live life again and again. Those who ride the River of Life return again and again in new flesh and new lives, the weight of their experience accumulating over the course of their many lives, drawing them ever closer to the truth and final absolution.

Those who follow the teachings of sangpotshi practice meditation not to escape from their bodies but to unite the elements of their being more fully, accepting and understanding the experience of life in its many facets. They recognize that suffering is the common lot in life. Evil practice strips away their experience, forcing them to live again until they have learned the proper lessons, and so they focus on a gentle but strong interaction with others. The River is different for everyone, but its destination is the same, and the River teaches tolerance for all. Followers of the River do not give way to enemies, but they rarely kill their foes, for the accumulation of life itself is suffering enough.

In a certain way, sangpotshi is a companion philosophy to Pao-Lung—where Pao-Lung teaches of the value of learning from the lives of your ancestors, Sangpotshi teaches the value of learning from your own previous lives. The greatest of philosophers have argued that these two philosophies, in the end, are the same.

## Tamashigo

There is no luck, good or bad—only the whims of the spirits on the road of destiny. Within each aspect of nature there resides a spirit or soul. Whether that spirit is inherent or whether it was placed there by a god is irrelevant: Everything has a spirit, and the spirits must be propitiated. Some of these aspects are physical, tangible things: waterfalls, mighty rivers, towering cliffs, magnificent trees. Others might be less tangible, such as the wind, sunset, or the smell of growing things. Still

## DEITIES OF TIAN XIA

| Deity | AL | Areas of Concern | Domains | Favored Weapon |
|---|---|---|---|---|
| Abadar | LN | cities, law, merchants, wealth | Earth, Law, Nobility, Protection, Travel | light crossbow |
| Daikitsu | N | agriculture, craftsmanship, kitsune, rice | Animal, Artifice, Community, Plant, Weather | flail |
| Desna | CG | dreams, luck, stars, travelers | Chaos, Good, Liberation, Luck, Travel | starknife |
| Fumeiyoshi | NE | dishonor, envy, graves, undead | Death, Destruction, Evil, Repose, War | naginata |
| General Susumu | LE | archery, horses, personal glory, war | Evil, Glory, Law, Nobility, War | longbow |
| Hei Feng | CN | sea, storms, thunder, wind | Air, Chaos, Destruction, Water, Weather | nine-ring broadsword |
| Irori | LN | history, knowledge, martial arts, self-perfection | Healing, Knowledge, Law, Rune, Strength | unarmed strike |
| Kofusachi | CG | abundance, discovery, happiness, prosperity | Chaos, Charm, Good, Luck, Travel | bo staff |
| Lady Nanbyo | CE | earthquakes, fire, plague, suffering | Chaos, Destruction, Evil, Fire, Plant | warhammer |
| Lamashtu | CE | demons, madness, monsters, nightmares | Chaos, Evil, Madness, Strength, Trickery | falchion |
| Lao Shu Po | NE | night, rats, thieves | Animal, Darkness, Evil, Luck, Trickery | dagger |
| Nalinivati | N | fertility, nagaji, snakes, sorcery | Charm, Magic, Nobility, Rune, Scalykind | urumi |
| Pharasma | N | birth, death, fate, prophecy | Death, Healing, Knowledge, Repose, Water | dagger |
| Qi Zhong | NG | healing, magic, medicine | Good, Healing, Knowledge, Magic, Protection | heavy mace |
| Shelyn | NG | art, beauty, love, music | Air, Charm, Good, Luck Protection | glaive |
| Shizuru | LG | ancestors, honor, the sun, swordplay | Glory, Good, Law, Repose, Sun | katana |
| Sun Wukong | CN | drunkenness, nature, trickery | Animal, Chaos, Liberation, Travel, Trickery | quarterstaff |
| Tsukiyo | LG | jade, the moon, spirits | Darkness, Good, Law, Madness, Repose | longspear |
| Yaezhing | LE | harsh justice, murder, punishment | Artifice, Death, Evil, Law, Trickery | shuriken |
| Yamatsumi | N | mountains, volcanoes, winter | Earth, Fire, Protection, Strength, Water | tetsubo |

others have no physical basis but are instead qualities: growth, industry, and right-mindedness, for example. When these spirits form physical bodies, they are known as kami, yet this ability does not make them anything less than spirits.

These spirits make themselves felt in ways both subtle and broad. They may cause bad luck or intercede with the gods for deserving mortals. They may warn of coming wars or illnesses, or may deliver these things themselves. To propitiate the spirits, the adherents of Tamashigo build personal shrines at home or ad-hoc shrines in places of great natural beauty, offering small gifts both for the sacred nature of the place and the spirits not acknowledged in other places. When given their proper fealty, these spirits help smooth one's daily life, and may even become valuable allies in the natural world. When ignored, nature itself is thought to rise against the transgressor.

## RELIGION

Just as in the lands of the Inner Sea, religion and faith play a vital role in the daily lives of the people of the Dragon Empires. And while there are deities and powerful extraplanar beings beyond count in search of followers, the faiths of 20 gods are particularly strong in Tian Xia.

## MAJOR DEITIES OF THE DRAGON EMPIRES

Most inhabitants of the Dragon Empires recognize 20 powerful deities in the pantheon of Tian Xia. While most of these religions come from Tian Xia or neighboring regions, six of them are also well known in the Inner Sea region. Note that several of the deities here have a nationality that includes "(Dragon)" and are often depicted in draconic forms or associate with imperial dragons.

### ABADAR, GOD OF WALLS AND DITCHES

LN god of cities, law, merchants, and wealth

**CLERICS**

**Domains** Earth, Law, Nobility, Protection, Travel
**Subdomains** Defense, Inevitable, Leadership, Martyr, Metal, Trade
**Favored Weapon** light crossbow

**FAITH**

**Sacred Animal** eagle; **Symbol** golden key

**Centers of Worship** Amanandar, Goka, Hongal, Lingshen, Shokuro, Xa Hoi

**Nationality** Taldan

Abadar is well known throughout Golarion—in Tian Xia, however, he is known as the god of Walls and Ditches, symbolizing humanity's penchant for transforming the land by simultaneously building upon it and taking away from it.

That walls and ditches can aid greatly in the defense of a city is seen as common sense as much as it is the teaching of Abadar. The god of cities and merchants, Abadar seeks to bring civilization to the frontiers of Golarion and wealth to all who support law. Most cities in Tian Xia have at least one temple or shrine to Abadar, calling on him to protect their cities and citizens and bring wealth to their coffers. His greatest temple in all the Dragon Empires—and perhaps in all the world—is in the bustling city-state of Goka. He is typically depicted in Tian artwork as a handsome and clean-shaven Tian-Shu man carrying a golden crossbow and wearing golden robes that are muddy along the lowest edges.

## DAIKITSU, LADY OF FOXES

N goddess of agriculture, craftsmanship, kitsune, and rice

### CLERICS

**Domains** Animal, Artifice, Community, Plant, Weather

**Subdomains** Construct, Family, Fur, Growth, Home, Seasons

**Favored Weapon** flail

### FAITH

**Sacred Animal** fox; **Symbol** nine-tailed fox

**Centers of Worship** Forest of Spirits, Minkai, Shokuro

**Nationality** Kitsune

Daikitsu is widely worshiped in Tian Xia, as she is the goddess of rice, a staple food in those lands, as well as of agriculture and craftsmanship. Farmers pray to Daikitsu for good harvests, smiths and craftsmen seek her blessing for their creations, and families ask for her protection for their homes and families. Known as the Lady of Foxes, Daikitsu usually appears as beautiful kitsune woman with snow-white fur and nine tails. She is also the patron of kitsune, who venerate her as the mother of their race.

## DESNA, GODDESS OF THE NORTH STAR

CG goddess of dreams, luck, stars, travelers

### CLERICS

**Domains** Chaos, Good, Liberation, Luck, Travel

**Subdomains** Azata, Curse, Exploration, Fate, Freedom, Revolution

**Favored Weapon** starknife

### FAITH

**Sacred Animal** butterfly; **Symbol** blue butterfly with stars, moon, and sun on its wings

**Centers of Worship** Forest of Spirits, Hongal, Hwanggot, Jinin, Kwanlai, Minata, Minkai, Nagajor, Shaguang, Tianjing, Wall of Heaven

**Nationality** Varisian

Desna, called the Goddess of the North Star in Tian Xia, is the goddess of dreams, stars, and luck. Clouds of butterflies

always accompany her. Long ago, Desna hung the stars in the sky and gifted mortals with the desire for mystery and travel. Adventurers, scouts, travelers, and wanderers all venerate her, and gamblers and thieves look to her for luck in their endeavors. Desna's faith reaches across Golarion, and while she remains strongly associated with Varisians and elves, among the Tians she is typically depicted as a beautiful, butterfly-winged Tian-Min woman.

## FUMEIYOSHI, LORD OF ENVY

NE god of dishonor, envy, graves, and undead

### CLERICS

**Domains** Death, Destruction, Evil, Repose, War

**Subdomains** Blood, Daemon, Souls, Rage, Tactics, Undead

**Favored Weapon** naginata

### FAITH

**Sacred Animal** wolf; **Symbol** red demonic face

**Centers of Worship** Chu Ye, Forest of Spirits, Minkai, Shenmen

**Nationality** Tian-Min

Fumeiyoshi is the Lord of Envy, the god of dishonor, envy, and graves. Originally the god of night and brother of the moon god Tsukiyo, Fumeiyoshi grew jealous of Shizuru's love for Tsukiyo and slew his brother in a fit of rage. When Shizuru returned Tsukiyo to life, she stripped Fumeiyoshi of his position and banished him to her brother's grave, decreeing that he would always envy his betters, as the restless dead do the living. Fumeiyoshi is considered the patron of oni and the undead, and of those paladins and samurai who have been dishonored or have fallen from grace. In lands where the dead are buried, people often make sacrifices to Fumeiyoshi as the god of graves to placate him into leaving deceased loved ones where they are laid to rest, lest they rise again as undead horrors. Fumeiyoshi has many forms, but most often manifests as a nearly skeletal humanoid with three eyes, jagged tusks, and twisted claws.

## GENERAL SUSUMU, THE BLACK DAIMYO

LE god of archery, horses, personal glory, and war

### CLERICS

**Domains** Evil, Glory, Law, Nobility, War

**Subdomains** Blood, Devil, Heroism, Honor, Leadership, Tactics

**Favored Weapon** longbow

### FAITH

**Sacred Animal** horse; **Symbol** black winged horse

**Centers of Worship** Chu Ye, Hongal, Kaoling, Minkai, Shokuro, Xa Hoi

**Nationality** Tian-Min (Dragon)

General Susumu, the Black Daimyo, is the half-brother of Shizuru, and the patron of those samurai more focused on

war and glory than honor and heroism. Widely worshiped in Hongal, Kaoling, Minkai, and Shokuro, he is the god of archery, horsemanship, and war. General Susumu leads a great army of samurai and warriors who died gloriously in battle, and has been known to appear at great conflicts, sometimes merely watching, and other times joining in for the sheer joy of fighting. In his humanoid form, General Susumu has red skin and great bristling eyebrows and wears ornate black o-yoroi armor. He rides a black winged horse into battle and carries an iron longbow that shoots arrows of fire. When his anger is truly roused, he appears as an immense crimson dragon with eyes of fire and obsidian tusks.

## HEI FENG, DUKE OF THUNDER

CN god of the sea, storms, thunder, and wind

**CLERICS**

**Domains** Air, Chaos, Destruction, Water, Weather

**Subdomains** Catastrophe, Cloud, Oceans, Protean, Storms, Wind

**Favored Weapon** nine-ring broadsword

**FAITH**

**Sacred Animal** raven; **Symbol** lightning bolt issuing from a black storm cloud

**Centers of Worship** Dtang Ma, Goka, Hwanggot, Kwanlai, Lingshen, Minata, Minkai, Wanshou, Xidao

**Nationality** Tengu

Hei Feng is the god of storms, wind, and the sea. Called the Duke of Thunder, Hei Feng is a deity of both the rain that makes crops grow and of the storms that destroy entire villages. He is god of the winds and currents that safely carry ships from one port to another and of the gales that drive ships off course and sink them to the bottom of the sea. The gentle tide that laps against the shore is under Hei Feng's purview, as is the tsunami that devastates the coastline. Farmers pray to Hei Feng for rain, and sailors make offerings to him for safe journeys. Hei Feng is the patron of the tengu race, and appears as a powerful tengu with smoking black feathers. He wields a nine-ring broadsword whose blade dances with lightning, and whose clashing rings create the thunder. Hei Feng is always accompanied by four divine servants known as the counts of wind, rain, thunder, and lightning, who ride storm clouds through the sky to carry out their master's bidding.

## IRORI, THE ENLIGHTENED ONE

LN god of history, knowledge, martial arts, and self-perfection

**CLERICS**

**Domains** Healing, Knowledge, Law, Rune, Strength

**Subdomains** Inevitable, Language, Memory, Resolve, Restoration, Thought

**Favored Weapon** unarmed strike

**FAITH**

**Sacred Animal** ox; **Symbol** blue hand inside a blue circle

**Centers of Worship** Amanandar, Goka, Hongal, Lingshen, Minkai, Quain, Wall of Heaven, Xa Hoi

**Nationality** Vudrani

Irori was a Vudrani man who achieved absolute physical and mental perfection and thus ascended to godhood. Known as the Enlightened One in the Dragon Empires, Irori is the god of history, knowledge, and inner strength. He is a tolerant deity, respectful of other faiths, and his worshipers practice this tolerance themselves. Many of Irori's followers are monks who seek to follow his path to ultimate self-perfection through meditation, physical exercise, and unarmed combat. Sages and scholars venerate Irori as well. Irori is rarely depicted in art, as his faithful believe no mere image can capture their god's perfection.

## KOFUSACHI, THE LAUGHING GOD

CG god of abundance, discovery, happiness, and prosperity

**CLERICS**

**Domains** Chaos, Charm, Good, Luck, Travel

**Subdomains** Azata, Exploration, Fate, Love, Lust, Trade

**Favored Weapon** bo staff

**FAITH**

**Sacred Animal** dog; **Symbol** string of seven coins

**Centers of Worship** Hongal, Hwanggot, Tianjing

**Nationality** Tian-Hwan

Kofusachi, the Laughing God, is the deity of happiness, prosperity, and abundance. His blessing is invoked when a child is born, at weddings, before business deals, and at the beginning of long journeys. He is depicted as a plump, bald man, always smiling, with bare, calloused feet, a walking stick in hand, and a dog at his heels. An incurable wanderer and inveterate libertine, Kofusachi has taken numerous gods and goddesses as lovers. Though his wanderlust always keeps such relationships from becoming too serious, Kofusachi is fast friends with Daikitsu, Desna, and Shelyn.

## LADY NANBYO, THE WIDOW OF SUFFERING

CE goddess of earthquakes, fire, plague, and suffering

**CLERICS**

**Domains** Chaos, Destruction, Evil, Fire, Plant

**Subdomains** Ash, Catastrophe, Decay, Demon, Rage, Smoke

**Favored Weapon** warhammer

**FAITH**

**Sacred Animal** crow; **Symbol** flaming rift in the earth

**Centers of Worship** Goka, Minata, Shaguang, Shenmen, Wanshou

**Nationality** Tian-Sing (Dragon)

Lady Nanbyo is the goddess of plague, fire, earthquakes, and other calamities. Even tsunamis and volcanic eruptions (usually the work of Hei Feng and Yamatsumi, respectively) are typically blamed on Lady Nanbyo, for she eagerly adds her own torments to such catastrophes and delights in the pain and suffering that follow in their wake. At the same time, however, people pray to Lady Nanbyo to spare them during such times of upheaval. Called the Widow of Suffering, Lady Nanbyo has been married many times, but all of her husbands have met terrible and tragic ends. While Lady Nanbyo can appear as a seductive woman when she wishes, her true form is said to be that of a ravenous, fire-breathing dragon with a dozen legs.

### LAMASHTU, GRANDMOTHER NIGHTMARE

CE goddess of demons, madness, monsters, and nightmares

**CLERICS**

**Domains** Chaos, Evil, Madness, Strength, Trickery

**Subdomains** Deception, Demon, Ferocity, Insanity, Nightmare, Thievery

**Favored Weapon** falchion

**FAITH**

**Sacred Animal** jackal; **Symbol** three-eyed jackal face

**Centers of Worship** Darklands, Goka, Nagajor, Shaguang, Valashmai Jungle, Wall of Heaven, Wanshou

**Nationality** Demon

Lamashtu, who is known as Grandmother Nightmare in Tian Xia, is the goddess of madness, monsters, and nightmares, and is widely worshiped by monstrous races across Golarion. Also the most powerful demon lord of the Abyss, jackal-headed Lamashtu has birthed countless horrors and monstrosities from her terrible womb, monsters that plague Golarion to this day. Lamashtu's followers seek out deformity and mutilation in both themselves and others, and the twisted human cultists who worship her practice their terrible rituals in secret. Her cultists can be found in most major cities, but are the most populous in wild lands like the Wall of Heaven or Valashmai Jungle, where the true monsters dwell.

### LAO SHU PO, OLD RAT WOMAN

NE goddess of night, rats, and thieves

**CLERICS**

**Domains** Animal, Darkness, Evil, Luck, Trickery

**Subdomains** Curse, Daemon, Fur, Loss, Night, Thievery

**Favored Weapon** dagger

**FAITH**

**Sacred Animal** rat; **Symbol** curled and emaciated rat

**Centers of Worship** Darklands, Goka, Kwanlai, Minata, Shenmen, Wanshou

**Nationality** Rat

Lao Shu Po, or Old Rat Woman, was not always a goddess. Once, long ago, she was simply a rat, skulking in the shadows. When Fumeiyoshi killed his brother Tsukiyo, Lao Shu Po crept into the moon god's grave to feed on Tsukiyo's corpse. She absorbed some of Tsukiyo's divine power, such that when Tsukiyo was returned to life and Fumeiyoshi was banished from heaven, she was able to steal the portfolio of night from Fumeiyoshi, becoming the goddess of night, thieves, and rats. Lao Shu Po is the patron of thieves and of many wayangs, who pray to her to hide their activities in the dark of night. Lao Shu Po appears as an old hag or as an immense, six-legged rat.

### NALINIVATI, THE SERPENT'S KISS

N goddess of fertility, nagaji, snakes, and sorcery

**CLERICS**

**Domains** Charm, Magic, Nobility, Rune, Scalykind

**Subdomains** Arcane, Divine, Leadership, Love, Lust, Wards

**Favored Weapon** urumi

**FAITH**

**Sacred Animal** snake; **Symbol** snake coiled in a lotus flower

**Centers of Worship** Dtang Ma, Nagajor, Xa Hoi, Xidao

**Nationality** Naga

Nalinivati was the legendary first queen of Nagajor, who gave birth to the varied naga races in ages past. A powerful sorceress, Nalinivati used her own sorcery to ascend to godhood. Called the Queen of Nagas, Nalinivati is the goddess of sorcery and snakes, and is the patron goddess of the nagaji. Also known as the Serpent's Kiss, Nalinivati is a goddess of fertility as well, and has been romantically linked with Daikitsu, though the two goddesses neither confirm nor deny the rumors. Her worship is most widespread in Nagajor, but sorcerers, nagas, smitten lovers, and snake cults throughout Tian Xia venerate her. Nalinivati appears as an immense naga with brilliantly colored hair and scales. She is often depicted in art as emerging from an egg, or as guarding a clutch of eggs.

### PHARASMA, MOTHER OF SOULS

N goddess of birth, death, fate, and prophecy

**CLERICS**

**Domains** Death, Healing, Knowledge, Repose, Water

**Subdomains** Ancestors, Ice, Memory, Resurrection, Souls, Thought

**Favored Weapon** dagger

## FAITH

**Sacred Animal** whippoorwill; **Symbol** spiral of energy

**Centers of Worship** Amanandar, Dtang Ma, Goka, Shaguang, Shenmen, Shokuro, Zi Ha

**Nationality** Garundi

Pharasma is the goddess of birth, death, and fate, and it is she who judges all mortals when they die, when their souls pass through her Boneyard. In the Dragon Empires, Pharasma is often called the Mother of Souls to honor her role as the giver of life and reaper of death. Since the beginning of the Age of Succession, Pharasma's Tian worshipers have focused less on her role as the goddess of prophecy, and most of her adherents now come from the ranks of expectant mothers, midwives, undertakers, and those who grieve for the recently departed. Pharasma despises undead creatures as abominations, and her worshipers seek to eradicate them whenever possible. Among the domains and subdomains that are granted by Pharasma are Death and Souls, but worshipers of Pharasma who choose either of these adjust the granted domain spells slightly. Those who choose the domain of Death replace *animate dead* with *speak with dead*, *create undead* with *antilife shell*, and *create greater undead* with *symbol of death*. Those who choose the Souls subdomain replace *animate dead* with *speak with dead*.

### QI ZHONG, MASTER OF MEDICINE

NG god of healing, magic, and medicine

#### CLERICS

**Domains** Good, Healing, Knowledge, Magic, Protection

**Subdomains** Agathion, Divine, Memory, Purity, Restoration, Resurrection

**Favored Weapon** heavy mace

#### FAITH

**Sacred Animal** crane; **Symbol** wagon wheel with spokes made of fire, earth, metal, water, and wood

**Centers of Worship** Jinin, Quain, Tianjing, Xidao, Zi Ha

**Nationality** Tian-Shu

Qi Zhong is the Master of Medicine, god of healing and magic. It was Qi Zhong, at Shizuru's bequest, who employed his skill and magic to bring the moon god Tsukiyo back to life after he was slain by his brother Fumeiyoshi, and it was Qi Zhong who first taught mortals the importance of the five elements—fire, earth, metal, water, and wood—and their connection to magic, medicine, and martial arts, among other pursuits. Healers, sages, scholars, and practitioners of traditional Tian medicine venerate Qi Zhong, as do wizards and mystic theurges, many of whom serve in his priesthood. Qi Zhong's faithful believe it is their duty to teach their knowledge and learning to others. He appears as a kindly older man dressed in a healer's robe that seems to shift between the five elements.

### SHELYN, LADY OF CHRYSANTHEMUMS

NG goddess of art, beauty, love, and music

#### CLERICS

**Domains** Air, Charm, Good, Luck, Protection

**Subdomains** Agathion, Cloud, Defense, Fate, Love, Purity

**Favored Weapon** glaive

#### FAITH

**Sacred Animal** songbird; **Symbol** songbird with rainbow-colored tail

**Centers of Worship** Hwanggot, Jinin, Minkai, Tianjing, Zi Ha

**Nationality** Taldan

Shelyn is the embodiment of love and art, beauty and music. Called the Lady of Chrysanthemums in Tian Xia, Shelyn is the patron of actors, geisha, and other entertainers, as well as of poets, writers, painters, and other artists. Her inspiration can be seen in a perfectly sublime haiku, an exquisitely displayed flower arrangement, or a flawlessly performed tea ceremony. Shelyn teaches that beauty comes from within and that love should not be solely carnal. She is frequently exasperated with Kofusachi and his more licentious attitudes toward love, but the two remain close friends. In art, Shelyn is presented as a beautiful human woman of varying ethnicity.

### SHIZURU, EMPRESS OF HEAVEN

LG goddess of ancestors, honor, the sun, and swordplay

#### CLERICS

**Domains** Glory, Good, Law, Repose, Sun

**Subdomains** Ancestors, Archon, Day, Heroism, Honor, Light

**Favored Weapon** katana

#### FAITH

**Sacred Animal** carp; **Symbol** katana in front of the sun

**Centers of Worship** Amanandar, Goka, Jinin, Minkai, Quain, Shokuro, Xa Hoi, Zi Ha

**Nationality** Tian-Min (Dragon)

Shizuru is the Empress of Heaven, goddess of ancestors and the sun. She is also the goddess of honor and swordplay, and is the patron of samurai and other honorable swordfighters. Shizuru loves the moon god Tsukiyo, so much so that she returned him to life when he was slain by his brother Fumeiyoshi. The two lovers are rarely together, however, just as night and day are forever divided, but the two deities are able to rejoin, if only briefly, during rare solar eclipses—a sacred time for both faiths. Shizuru's worship is popular throughout the Dragon Empires, but her faith is strongest in Minkai, for the emperors of that land revere Shizuru as their divine ancestor. Shizuru is often depicted in art as a beautiful samurai, as a magnificent dragon with golden scales, or as both simultaneously.

## SUN WUKONG, THE MONKEY KING

CN god of drunkenness, nature, and trickery

### CLERICS

**Domains** Animal, Chaos, Liberation, Travel, Trickery

**Subdomains** Deception, Exploration, Freedom, Protean, Revolution, Thievery

**Favored Weapon** quarterstaff

### FAITH

**Sacred Animal** monkey; **Symbol** stone monkey

**Centers of Worship** Forest of Spirits, Goka, Hwanggot, Kwanlai, Minata, Quain

**Nationality** Monkey

Sun Wukong, the Monkey King, is a trickster god, famous in tales throughout the Dragon Empires. Once a stone statue of a monkey given life, Sun Wukong was made the king of all monkeys, but he wanted more. He sought out the god of magic, Qi Zhong, hoping to obtain the secret of immortality. The Master of Medicine was unwilling to part with that secret, but he did teach Sun Wukong many magic powers. Eventually, Sun Wukong traveled to Pharasma's Boneyard and erased his name from her records, thus gaining immortality. The Monkey King is a notorious drunkard, and likes nothing more than strong alcohol, beautiful women, and wild brawls. Of all the Tian gods, Sun Wukong spends the most time wandering the Material Plane, drinking, carousing, and fighting, often in the guise of a drunken human martial artist.

## TSUKIYO, PRINCE OF THE MOON

LG god of the jade, moon, and spirits

### CLERICS

**Domains** Darkness, Good, Law, Madness, Repose

**Subdomains** Ancestors, Archon, Insanity, Moon, Night, and Souls

**Favored Weapon** longspear

### FAITH

**Sacred Animal** hare; **Symbol** jade crescent moon

**Centers of Worship** Goka, Jinin, Minkai, Nagajor, Tianjing, Wall of Heaven, Zi Ha

**Nationality** Tian-Min

Tsukiyo is the god of jade, the moon, and spirits. He is the brother of Fumeiyoshi, the god of envy, and lover of the sun goddess Shizuru. Called the Prince of the Moon, Tsukiyo was slain by his jealous brother, and it is said that Shizuru's tears, mingled with Tsukiyo's blood, formed the first stones of jade, which remains sacred to the moon god's faith. Tsukiyo was returned to life by Shizuru, and upon his rebirth, he acquired the portfolio of spirits and became patron of the reincarnated samsaran race. His worship is popular in the Forest of Spirits, and his shrines can often be found attached to larger temples to Shizuru.

## YAEZHING, MINISTER OF BLOOD

LE god of harsh justice, murder, and punishment

### CLERICS

**Domains** Artifice, Death, Evil, Law, Trickery

**Subdomains** Construct, Deception, Devil, Murder, Toil, Undead

**Favored Weapon** shuriken

### FAITH

**Sacred Animal** tiger; **Symbol** bloody shuriken

**Centers of Worship** Goka, Kaoling, Lingshen, Nagajor

**Nationality** Tian-Shu

Yaezhing is the god of murder and death. But as the Minister of Blood, he is also the punisher of the gods, the enforcer of divine justice. His dual roles sometimes conflict with one another, as when Yaezhing had to carry out Shizuru's punishment against Fumeiyoshi, who had murdered his brother Tsukiyo. This duality is also reflected in Yaezhing's temples, where his priests are often contracted to mete out punishments for convicted criminals, but are also available for murder for hire. Yaezhing is the patron of ninja and assassins, but he is also worshiped by executioners, judges, and those constables for whom inflicting punishment is more important than determining guilt. He appears as a shadowy humanoid figure swathed in darkness. His head is that of a tiger with human eyes.

## YAMATSUMI, THE MOUNTAIN LORD

N god of mountains, volcanoes, and winter

### CLERICS

**Domains** Earth, Fire, Protection, Strength, Water

**Subdomains** Ash, Caves, Defense, Ice, Resolve, Smoke

**Favored Weapon** tetsubo

### FAITH

**Sacred Animal** ram; **Symbol** snow-capped erupting volcano

**Centers of Worship** Dtang Ma, Hongal, Minkai, Nagajor, Wall of Heaven, Zi Ha

**Nationality** Tian-Min

Yamatsumi is the god of mountains, volcanoes, and winter. Every snow-capped mountain peak is a temple to him, and every volcanic eruption a sign of his wrath. Yet Yamatsumi is also a god of renewal, for his winter snows feed the rivers running through green valleys, and ash from his volcanoes fertilizes the fields of farmers. Ascetic mountain monks, or yamabushi, make up a majority of his faithful, but people from all walks of life pray to Yamatsumi to avert his wrath when the first winds of winter blow, or the nearby volcano belches smoke. Yamatsumi appears as a giant man with ice for skin, lava for hair and a beard, and two pairs of ram's horns on his head.

# The Inner Sea World Guide

## Golarion Needs Heroes... Be One!

The perfect world guide for Pathfinder RPG players and Game Masters alike, this definitive 320-page full-color hardcover volume contains expanded coverage of more than 40 nations, details on gods, religions, and factions, new character options, monsters, and more. Chart the events of your Pathfinder campaign with a beautiful poster map that reveals the lands of the Inner Sea region in all their treacherous glory!

## AVAILABLE NOW!

paizo.com